Margaret,

TIME SHIFT

God Bless You!

...THE PARADIGM

Thank You for getting Time Shift!
Buckle up! It is a ride + a ½!

Robbie Thomas

[signature]

Published by

Robbie Thomas Offices

Copyright ©2012 by Robbie Thomas

ISBN-13: 978-1477433928

ISBN-10: 1477433929

Robbie Thomas

Acknowledgements

First and foremost I want to give thanks to God, who guides me throughout my day! I draw my strength through thought and prayer all day long and from the fire within.

My family who puts up with me with everything I do in life and still haven't disowned me. We laugh, work hard together, share in everything in life. This is my core to whom I am.

My beautiful wife whom I owe everything to for without you, I literally am just a man in an empty shell. Your compassion and understanding is beyond this world, you are my Angel!

My children who keep me busy with everything they do, I so love you. I look into your eyes seeing promise, hope, love and a world of so much expression of who you really are its amazing! You are the keepers of my soul!

Thank you Jessie for the beautiful design art work of the book. You are my Angel and I love you!

Thank you Scott Alan Roberts, for the most revered forward you created from your heart and thoughts. I am more than happy to call you friend, thank you brother!

Thank you to all those who have reviewed this book, and giving your personal thoughts and feelings, on what is written. It's the Critic that gives the direction, which is greatly appreciated

To my personal Spiritual teachers, each day I grow so much more in your

Robbie Thomas

guidance learning each day that there is a difference in making that difference. Thank You!

I like to thank all of you who are reading this now, may you be blessed beyond imagination. You make this possible for me to keep doing what I do; I send you many blessings always!

A special thanks to our ancestors, who have come before all of us as many notations throughout the centuries have been left as lessons, or let's say, the writing on the wall. Thank You.

Robbie Thomas

Forward

If you are anything like me, you have found yourself in awe of Robbie Thomas. I first encountered him back in my days with the Ghost Hunters as editor-in-chief of their official publication, TAPS ParaMagazine. It took only a few minutes before he unwittingly revealed himself as one of the most completely genuine, authentically gifted intuitive I had ever met. Belying his gruff exterior and black-tee-shirt-clad, dew-rag-wear in' biker persona, I found Robbie to be a soft spoken, gentle giant of a man who not only had the ability to bombast when needed, but that rare gift to see the Other Side. There are many who make the claim, but few who have the Sight. Robbie Thomas is a gifted man with erudite perceptions. He is also a man who possesses that certain brand of altruism that places helping others above monetary gain, and he has worked closely with individuals and law enforcement officials many times over to resolve the otherwise un-resolvable.

While I have an understanding of how the mechanics of the psychic phenomena works, I will admittedly be one of the many who stand in front of my own office window, gazing out at the world, daydreaming of the good, the bad and the ugly, but cannot ever claim to have a clear vision of what is to come. While I see politics and consequences, actions and reactions in real time, I can only make educated guesses as to what will follow in their natural courses. Robbie experiences a deeper Sight that reveals motive, character, causality and effect, and ultimately a glimpse – sometimes coming in scattered movie-like clips – of the things unseen and the outcomes of human behaviour, decadence, evolution and entropic, fate-laced

Robbie Thomas

happenstances. He is a man of rare gift.

While most of us walk around in a haze regarding the plethora of prophecies and myriad miasmic motifs of the End of Days, Robbie Thomas is given real flashes in real time of things that are unfolding. And, sometimes, he doesn't even recognize it at the time it is being delivered. He suffers from the debilitation of being Human, which sometimes clouds the pictures and leaves even him wondering what it is he just saw. At times he is reduced to tears upon the realization that something he saw was very much more than the stuffs of his imaginations and contemplative daydreaming, and he wonders why he didn't make the connections that were delivered. This drives him to pursue even greater excellence and understanding, straining through the diaphanous to lay hands on the tangible and efficacious. Even a gifted, psychic intuitive needs to process the images he is given, and sometimes he has to just go with the message that is delivered, eschewing the desire to doubt and analyze. And in so doing, Robbie has to become that paradoxical hinge-pin that exists in the here and now, yet lives in a world that reveals so much more. The responsibility can be staggering for any individual; the strain on the soul monumental.

Robbie Thomas has taken us on journeys of discovery many times over, as in his books Paranormal Encounters, and A Link to Heaven: Chats with the Other Side, but for the first time ever, he has moulded his visions, crafting those delivered messages into a fictional tale wrapped around the doom of mankind. Leaning heavily on the Mayan prophecies of the end of humanity and the destruction of the earth, Robbie takes us on a round-the-world jaunt, peeking into the lives of the individuals caught in the impending disaster, and the cloistered rooms of governments as they find themselves suddenly facing what they can only describe as 'Doomsday.' With the verve and panache of the brand of science fiction movie you grew up watching as a kid, Time Shift carries you through the swiftly encroaching events of an earth-wide crisis via the experiences of normal people. Two history professors, an archaeologist, several arctic geologists, a mid-western mayor and his sheriff all offer up the destruction of the world as seen through their intimate circumstances. From ruined Mayan temples to the decks of US naval aircraft carriers; from the halls of the Kremlin to the Oval Office, Robbie brings you into the intimate circles of those who are experiencing what could be their last day on Earth.

Good science fiction seems always to be imbued with philosophical calls to action ranging from brief morality plays to sophisticated dissertations. Robbie Thomas does not break that rule. If only as a vehicle to transport a message, Robbie's delve into fiction delivers a heartfelt, soulful impact that at once vilifies and rectifies, yet ultimately unifies.

Never view prophecies of the end of the world as anything short of divine taps on the shoulder, and a brass-blown Reverie to the galloping soul.

Scott Alan Roberts

May 7, 2012

New Richmond, WI, USA

Robbie Thomas

Time Shift – The Paradigm

www.scottalanroberts.com

www.intrepidmag.com

www.paradigmsymposium.com

Robbie Thomas

Prelude Time Shift…The Paradigm

Civilization as we know it has come to a fork in the road. One path leads to obliteration, while the other, more challenging path is simply the desire to live. The world has for centuries ignored the coming of what has been predicted by scholars and prophets. The time has come for the wrongful actions man has created to be judged accordingly. The creation of everything stares a dark abyss of no return in the face. New York City is in total annihilation with destruction all around. Fires rage while black smoke fills the air. The eerie sound of silence that lingers stretches throughout the chaos of despair. The wake of destruction quickly changes to the empty streets of Washington D.C., where nothing moves while the feeling of emptiness fills the echoes of the hallowed once busy metropolis.

The capital building lay in ruins, while the White House that once stood for strength, is now bowing in devastation, the tattered American Flag wages war on its own flapping in the wind, barely hanging on the pole in the front yard. Philadelphia the city of freedom stands in total seclusion destroyed from the wrath of end times. The Liberty Bell is now broken into two as the buildings that shadowed over it are now nothing but rubble. Japan has been devoured by a 9.0 earthquake that produced a monster Tsunami, which swept across the nation swallowing it whole taking everything within its sights into the dark waters. Nothing survived the horror that raged over the country leaving no signs of life, nothing whatsoever. The ravenous wave made its way across the ocean to encounter the west coast of Canada, the United States and as far south as the country of Peru.

Devastation roared throughout the awaiting countries, while the sounds of

Robbie Thomas

Time Shift – The Paradigm

the darkest days have arisen from the depths. Volcanoes spew fireballs, with walls

of fire that engulf much of the landscape of motherland of Russia, Asia and parts of

Europe, devouring everything in its path. Charred ruins lay resting where once stood

many cities along with its people who lived there. Nothing escapes the wrath,

nothing at all. The end times have come, could man have changed the course of

action of what has happened? Could mankind have altered the outcome of the

"Revelation 2012? What has been set in stone, is the roadmap of destruction for the

human race, it now begins with Time Shift, The Paradigm!

Robbie Thomas

Authors Note

Through life we have many coincidences that happen to us. It's in those times we must realize, what may come from one's collective thoughts, feelings or even in the form of a premonition, does indeed actually happen. In part of the explanation in the Prelude where the tragedy of March 11, 2011 occurred off the coast of Japan, this was discussed in private with a producer while writing a movie script and partially written about on my Facebook page days before it actually did happen. I want to extend my deepest sympathy towards all involved in this tragedy. In no shape or forum would I want to utilize this happening to further myself, as I have had much turmoil including it in this book from the script that was written. In some capacity within my soul, I know that the truth is the truth and in saying this, I want to keep the proper context of what has transpired days before the tragedy by honouring those who passed on that dreadful day. I have changed the location of the travesty making it more fictional. May God Bless Them All.

Robbie Thomas

Collaboration Validation

In early 2011, Robbie and I were discussing his movie scripts for his Psychic Nightmare Trilogy. He mentioned to me he was writing a new script that had an end of times theme to it. It was a worldwide apocalypse with catastrophic events in Peru, United States, and Japan. On March 10, 2011 in a telephone conversation, Robbie described for me the turbulent end-of-the world events contained in the writings, which included a giant tsunami caused by a nine point zero (9.0) earthquake. I thought nothing of it until Robbie and I talked two days later after the event in Japan. Imagine my surprise when the eight point nine (8.9) earthquake that caused the tsunami that hit Japan was reclassified as a nine point zero (9.0) earthquake. It is either a remarkable coincidence or a premonition written by Robbie and discussed with me just a day before it actually happened.

Remarkable!~ Don Hutcheson, Creative Producer, Liftoph Productions

Preface

Can you imagine sitting writing a movie script, which has a taste of adventure, the thrill ride of much suspense, many aspects of destruction, yet there is a tapping on your shoulder with the urgency to get it done? We all have seen the end of time movies that have your so called "hero" emerge in the end, or fate of a nation, where the people come together to overcome whatever it is that has descended upon them. Well, I wanted to add a bit more flavour in the direction of an entire global event, or several elements that take place at the same time, keeping the suspense at a real nail biter. I tried to look beyond your fatal plane crash, normal volcano, or small city earthquake, to really take a bite out of the old and spit out a new. So this way, the viewer would walk away thinking twice if it really could happen in ordinary life, plus, add a scale that would be unimaginable for most. I wrote a few notes trying to collage many different ideas, creating scenario's of science fiction to horror. Nevertheless, nothing really intrigued me much less captured my real inner feeling of that shock and awe grab. While creating many images in my mind of what others might like to see, or even putting myself in others shoes so to speak, there was really nothing I could conjure up that might put something over the top. Where am I going to get my idea? Where is that thought of cascading a real tragedy, married with catastrophe, that would be an "edge of your seat, want to see more" script?

I considered many things, and then it really hit me! I've had personal visions of many tragedies over the years, which many were either documented or collaborated with colleagues before they actually happened. This is what I was looking for! This is what people would like to see, and know if it could really

Robbie Thomas

happen to them. Yes, I finally had the edge. I had my script starting to take shape as the ideas finally started to flow from many years of seeing things. I decided to write about a super earthquake while literally giving it a 9.0 in the pacific not far from Japan. Staring out my office window, I've seen these events unfold, all the while passing them off as daydreams that were nothing more than the start of a really good script. As more fascinating scenes continued to flow, I kept the pen to paper writing every thought that emerged from my mind. I incorporated volcanoes at an enormous magnitude, where fireballs streaked across the sky while walls of fire engulfed small cities. Now we are getting somewhere, but where are we heading? Oh, I had much more rolling through all the thoughts that were painting themselves throughout my mindset, yet how was I to incorporate them in a strategic way that would unleash one of the world's wildest end of times scripts? A Tsunami! Yes of course! I couldn't have a super earthquake in the Pacific without a monster Tsunami bearing down on not just Japan, but also America, Canada and Peru. This was more than impressive for a fictional movie script dealing with so much going on at once. I also had to introduce a supernatural element to the entire scope of why this was taking place, then reflect to many possible predictions throughout the centuries that have kept man in the wings waiting to see if fulfillment of those so called etched in stone prophecies would come true.

During the writing of the script *Time Shift*, while posting on my own Facebook page as well as having a follow up phone conversation with two film producers, there was breaking news all over the television. Japan had been hit by a 8.9 magnitude Earthquake, which produced a Tsunami and it was now ravaging the country. This brought flashes going through my mind, I gasped looking at my wife as we both realized, "this couldn't be happening!" It was being played out all over the news, exactly as I wrote only days earlier and posting about it one day prior to the event. My heart fell to the floor. I was dumbfounded to see this, as many people in real life were losing their lives to a devastation that I thought was only fallacy on paper. Then the news broke once more! It wasn't an 8.9, it was a 9.0, exactly as I had written which really put everything into perspective. Was I, or have I been given a vision only days prior as I began the writing of the movie script on March 2nd 2011? Once again, I had also collaborated with two colleagues about this movie script including the 9.0 earthquake and tsunami on March 10th 2011, along with all the destruction that was now on the news globally. Here is the supernatural element I was looking for! Here is that edge of your seat nail biter that would grip everyone who watched this movie. Except it really did happen from a vision in writing only days prior. This most certainly is a prelude as well as a caution for all in this life as I kept pen to paper and now we enter …*Time Shift!*

Robbie Thomas

Introduction

Is it the ignorance of man or the desire to believe in what the future may hold that intrigues the very soul? Could it be the perception in one's mindset that the end is inevitable and written in stone for us all? There are those who would argue both sides of the table on this discussion, for what has been predetermined in quatrains or scriptures from the pen of a man centuries ago, might dictate an outcome of mankind today. The twist of fate or "something wicked this way comes," has always been a fan favourite among those who seek the thrill behind smoke and mirrors, or could this be real? Could we all be living in a paradigm predetermined, or are we just acting out what has been written in a script for the final act?

As man awaits his final days, he sits pondering what may lie in the shadows as the sand in the hourglass trickle away, leaving him wondering what fate waits in his last hours. The reality of living is that death is part of the equation while the uncertain is most certain. Many prophets, seers, as well as historians, have researched and documented over the centuries that the end times for mankind lay ahead. Destiny they say, is the accomplishment of your will to accept what will be, however, it is also how one can control this throughout their life, or do you? Has man really found the hourglass upon which one could look into seeing the future? If so, then what -if anything- does it truly hold for us all? Many questions like these are the plague upon which centuries of writings along with prophesied events are passed down to future generations. The end is near, yes indeed it is! What they didn't tell you! All the predictions along with the stories passed down, they got it WRONG! Just when you thought it safe, the end has come to claim the hour

Robbie Thomas

Time Shift – The Paradigm

unknown...Time Shift!

Robbie Thomas

Schools In!

September is a busy time of the year for Trinity Massachusetts, as the uptown area embraces the day with students from all over the world come together to seek knowledge in the many different studies offered at Winston University. While the wind blows during a fall day, sounds of the busy campus come alive with upbeat students making their way to their dorms and classes of study. The courtyard is busy with people milling about greeting each other as a new semester is about to begin. The excitement in the air is felt as many in this sleepy little community realize the rebirth of students and faculty members that are about to embark on a fresh year ahead of them.

The office of the Mayor has organized a homecoming of sorts for the senior class that will be graduating this year. Along with the Mayor's office the University will be overlooking all the events scheduled for the forthcoming graduates. All preparations are now in full motion with many special guest speakers being added to the celebrity presentation list. This is a huge time of year for Winston University, working hand in hand with the Mayor's office in preparation for a grand finale, which has proven to be one of the high points of the year for the little town!

All the towns' folks along with the small businesses in the area, openly welcome back all the students for the upcoming school year. Business seems to thrive very much from the many that will be now encompassing the campus of this historical town.

The historical University of Winston, sits upon a hilltop that once overlooked a battleground of the Civil War, which is now a national memorial park

Robbie Thomas

honouring those who once fought for freedoms and rights. The long winding road that leads to the beautiful campus grounds along with the lavish architecture of the university is simply breath taking during the fall. The campus is cascaded with beautiful gardens with stations marked out in story telling plaques that explain the history in which the University stands now. The entrance to the school has much grandeur with sophistication that is reflective to the prestigious academics this institution offers.

The voice of Professor David Gates can be heard speaking on ancient civilizations in the history class in room 132, as the Mayan era is the topic of discussion on opening day.

"So, all you highly educated protégés of mine. Who can tell me the name of the underworld god the Mayans called the god of death?" Professor Gates slowly walks around his class looking at the students. "Hmmm...Anyone? How about you Ms. Smith? Can you enlighten us on the knowledge, which I hope you all have retained since last semester in this class?"

Light laughter breaks out among the class from the friendly banter the Professor engages with his students. A less shy student named Jake speaks up with a grin on his face. "This should be interesting!" Jake slouches in his seat looking at Jenny Smith.

Jenny quickly turns with a sarcastic look on her face, peering back at Jake. She shifts in her seat lending a bit more persuasion to her follow up remark. "Careful Jake! If memory serves me right, your marks last semester, well, they seem to precede you right now."

Robbie Thomas

Time Shift – The Paradigm

The class erupts into laughter as Jake is put into his place. Jake looks back at Jenny with the shear grin of approval of what she just exploded upon his ego.

Professor Gates quickly interjects as laughter in the room is focused on Jake. He slowly walks over to where Jake is sitting, glances around the room, pauses for a moment before speaking while looking at his student and softly speaks. "Ok, Mr. Mara. As the day will have it, you have managed to creep your way into the conversation. I wonder, what the Mayans do with a poor soul like yourself? Let's see. Death...perhaps! No, that would be too easy. Let me see." Professor Gates quickly walks up to the front of the class, grabbing a small glass case filled with fire ants, turns and slowly paces back towards Jake. "What would the Mayans have in store for Jake, class? They might have tied you to a tree, smothered you with the sweet nectar of some fruit, allowing the fire ants to have their way with you. Yes, that is probably what they would have done." Professor Gates places the small glass case on Jake's desk and continues to make light of the situation. "Better yet, they might have taken you and made an offering to the sun god by chopping your head off!"

Professor Gates dramatically describes the fate of Jake as the class breaks out in laughter. Once again, Professor Gates makes light of the situation bringing the class everyone talks about to an enjoyable level of learning. He immediately walks over to the chalkboard, grabs a piece of chalk and begins to draw while writing the fate of Jake on its very black surface. He details the outcome that perhaps would be the end of civilization of Jake and what Jake has come to know as himself.

Jenny quickly joins in on the tormenting of Jake and she joins in on the

Robbie Thomas

theatrics. "Well Professor, that would be the only hot thing he would have, that's for sure! Even better having his head served on a platter, now that might be more intriguing!" Jenny looks sarcastically at Jake and winks.

Professor Gates laughs looking around the room. "Without further ado... Ms. Smith, the floor is yours madam. Please enlighten us, or at least poor old Jake here."

Jenny smiles looking at Jake, as she stands pacing slowly among the students who are now tentatively listening to the demise through her words.

"Professor if memory serves me right, the Mayans had many gods from the underworld. They all had many different purposes for many different ceremonies performed by the temple priests. However, the one I think you're alluding to would be called 'Kisin' the god of death... the stinking one!" Jenny quickly turns looking directly at Jake with a quirky smile on her face. "Oh and Professor, Kisin was also one of the most feared gods of that era. For if anyone whatsoever made fun or light of its power, the temple priests would have the head of the individual immediately severed from their body, stuck on a spear, then planted in front of the ceremonial steps leading to the temple." Jenny walks close to where Jake is sitting, leans over looking him in the eyes as she is finishing her statement about the Mayans. "They did this as a reminder not to make fun of his power within the community of the Mayan."

Professor Gates walks over to his desk sits on the edge of it, puts his hand to his face looking at the class. "Ahh, yes Ms. Smith, I think your right! It did have that familiar odour to it didn't it! See class, even back then they had their little stinkers, or at least named a god after one."

Robbie Thomas

Time Shift – The Paradigm

The conversation has now enticed Beth, Jenny's good friend as she lends her two cents and observations. " Professor, you be getting all up in Jake's space, you better be careful, he just might let off some of his death god stink on you."

Jake smiles, leans forward on his desk looking directly at Beth. He takes a deep breath and exhales. He slowly reaches for a piece of candy she has sitting on the top of her desk, places it in his mouth and winks. "Great, another freaking comedian emerges from the great history class of Professor Mayan Gates. How classic!"

Professor Gates with a smile from all the interaction taking place, walks to the middle of the class, turns putting his hand on Jakes shoulder and with a dark sinister voice, makes light once again of the entire situation. "Ok all my Mayan minuets! The day is about to come to a close here, so for the weekend the Mayan are wanting you to write us a five hundred word essay on the underworld and the gods from the underworld."

Moans erupt from the class on the announcement of the task at hand. Professor Gates quickly states. "Yes ok, entertain me. Its only five hundred words gang, give me a break. That's nothing compared to the amount of smack you all talk up half the time."

Jake walks over to where Jenny is standing waiting to talk to Professor Gates. "Great, there goes my serious make out session I had scheduled with Jenny, professor. You're ruining my life!"

Professor Gates looks at Jake with a grin. "By the look on her face Jake, the only make out session you're getting is self-administered. Even that is giving you

Robbie Thomas

Time Shift – The Paradigm

too much credit."

The bell rings as the students are gathering their books. The excitement of the weekend finally arriving can be felt as the students are leaving the class. Professor Gates reiterates about the assignment he just handed out. "Ok guys be good and remember, five hundred words by Monday. That's five hundred words! Don't forget, or some underworld god will get you. Be safe have a great weekend!"

As the milling about of students quickly disperse from the class, Jenny stays behind to ask Professor Gates a question about the Mayan people. She is vastly intrigued about the entire civilization as she desires more knowledge of that era.

"Professor I have a question for you. Wasn't there a paper, or some record from an archaeological dig a few years back? They dug up some tablets near one of the forbidden temples that had a warning of future events to happen I think. Something that was to be the pre-empt to 2012, like a prediction or something?"

Once again, Jenny's boyfriend Jake interrupts as he is anxious to get out of the class. "Come on Jen, the only thing being pre-empted is the fact of our quiet weekend together because we have this assignment now."

Jenny looks at Jake with a serious tone addressing his smite remark. "Oh give it a rest will you Jake. I am serious about this, even if you're not. Sorry professor sometimes he just has his head full of himself, you know what I mean?"

Professor Gates smiles as he looks at the two standing in front of him. He pauses for a moment to think. "That's ok Jenny, but your right. There were sacred tablets of warning that were dug up not long ago and now that I think of it-." Professor Gates walks around to the drawers on his desk and begins to riffle through

Robbie Thomas

them. "It was only up until recent we didn't understand exactly what they meant. I know I have a paper here of the research done on that dig. Ah yes, here it is! This is what some of my colleagues came up with while trying to read the hieroglyphics"

Another school staff member knocks on the open door to the class room interrupting the three talking, to remind Professor Gates of his meeting he has to be at. He points to his watch on his wrist. "Excuse me! Sorry for interruption David. Just thought I would remind you, we have that 4:30 meeting."

Professor Gates looks at his watch. "No, not a problem Michael. You're not interrupting, we were just finishing up. I am just going to finish up here and join you in a few." Professor Gates leans forward whispering to both Jenny and Jake. "He gets really grumpy if I am late for anything." The three smile at one another looking at Professor Write.

Professor Michael Wright smiles back tapping his watch. "You bet. See you in a few. Don't be late!" He continues to talk as he walks down the hallway. "You know how hard it is to get any time with you for anything anymore."

The three continue talking while Professor Gates gathers his things for the meeting. "Well you two, I better be off. I don't want to keep Professor Wright waiting. He seems to turn into an over ripen pumpkin that's cranky if I am late for meetings. It's just one of those things when you get old like him."

Jenny smiles and starts to push Jake out of the class. "Thanks Professor for your time. We have to be going as well. Have a great weekend! Let's catch up with Beth. Bye Professor." Jenny and Jake start to walk out of the class as Jake puts his arm around her.

Robbie Thomas

Time Shift – The Paradigm

Professor Gates gathers his things looking back at Jenny and Jake waving his hand saying goodbye. "Yes, you too guys. Have a good weekend. Oh and Jake, before you go. I look forward to reading your paper. I'm sure it will be filled with many moments of intrigue." Professor Gates smiles and laughs to himself. "Bye guys!"

Jake looks back at Professor Gates and smiles as he walks out the class room with Jenny. "So, what are the plans Jen? You're not really going to study all weekend are you? Come on! We have a fantastic weekend ahead of us."

Jenny and Jake start walking down the hall. Suddenly, Jenny stops. Slowly walks close to Jake, looking him in the eyes like a young innocent little girl. "Well Jake, I know my plans. It's going to be so much fun doing research on the Mayans, but it seems you have your own already. It looks like you will be having a party for one."

Jenny walks even closer to Jake now, snuggles up to him and in a sarcastic tone touching his hair. "If I were you and the way the Professor was looking at you, I would get that paper done for Monday. Just saying!"

Jake looks down at the floor knowing Jenny is right. "Yah, whatever! But next weekend you owe me!"

Professor Gates is now finally meeting up with Professor Wright at their late Friday afternoon special drinking hole. "Hey Michael! Sorry I'm late. My students, great bunch of kids they are. Though my one student Jenny Smith, nice girl and all, but she really takes this end of the world thing so serious with the Mayan. You know what I mean? It's almost like she believes something is truly about to happen to the

Robbie Thomas

entire human race with an end of the world scenario."

Professor Wright smiles as Professor Gates as he sits down. "They're kids David, young, inquisitive, wanting to know everything. You were like that once, or have you gotten that old on us now?" Michael looks for the waitress and waves her over. "Hell, I remember a young, soon-to-be professor Gates. He was a young student well into his studies many moons ago, who couldn't get enough of the theory behind all the ancient civilizations and predicted accounts"

Professor Gates sets his briefcase down, leans back in his chair looking with a grin at Professor Wright. He looks at the waitress standing there waiting to take their order. "You're right! Besides if they didn't ask me questions, I would be thinking something was wrong."

The waitress looks at both gentlemen. "Long day Professors?" She places two small napkins on the table in front of the two for their drinks.

David smiles. "Yes you can say that Sue, you can say that for sure. I'll have a scotch on the rocks please. Oh, make it a double will you! I feel a bit thirsty today."

The Waitress hands Professor Wright a menu. "Would you gentlemen like something to eat as well, or are we just keeping it strictly liquid today?"

David isn't ready for something to eat so he leans back in his chair thinking. "No, nothing for me Sue, just keep those drinks coming. It's been one of those days." David loosens his tie and unbuttons the top button on his shirt.

Michael looks at the menu then hands it back to the waitress. "I think I'll keep it a liquid meeting for now too Sue. Thank you anyway." He hands the waitress back the menu. "You know David perhaps a vacation is in order. You worked all summer long without any time off whatsoever, your showing signs of it my friend."

The waitress turns and begins to walk away. "Ok, two double scotches coming up!"

As the waitress walks away to get the drinks, Michael throws the newspaper on the table in front of him for David to look at. "Have you seen this yet? Something big is going on in South America David. Not only that, but things, strange things, happening in Europe as well." Michael sits forward in his chair looking around the room to see if anyone is listening in on their conversation while trying to keep it quiet. "The Pentagon is in high emergency mode, the state department has deployed troops to the South America region on standby!"

With a baffled look on his face David picks up the newspaper. "What's going on Michael?" David begins to focus on the lead story in the paper as he sits up in his chair.

Michael takes a drag from his cigarette. "My sources tell me some type of disturbance has occurred in Peru. It's early, but the details seem to be pointing towards some type of seismic activity. More than your little bump in the night type thing." Michael again looks around the room continuing to speak with David. "I know this might seem like a lot I'm throwing at you, but it has reached higher powers who have asked for assistance."

David reads the newspaper intensely, and then lowers it to look at Michael. "Peru? The only thing we know of in Peru are the new finds of the tribal routes and structured roads that were buried from long ago. Wasn't Elizabeth on that? Wasn't

Robbie Thomas

that her find?" David throws the paper on the table with the lead story face down.

Professor Wright pushes his glasses up on the bridge of his nose, sits back in his chair looking at David. "Yes, Elizabeth is the source. She is still down there researching when all this happened. He again sits forward in his chair taking a serious tone looking at Professor Gates. "David, she said something transpired that not even I can think possible. Being a physicist, I would have never thought something like this would ever occur."

Michael sits back once again in his chair as the waitress comes back with their drinks placing them on the table. The two professor's pause as the silence becomes loud about the topic of discussion. David leans forward and whispers, "What happened, Michael? Was anyone hurt? Did Elizabeth explain what happened?!"

"Yes, yes…she is fine! She was right there when this happened. She said the ground shook like something she has never seen before. Then as suddenly it started, it stopped!" Michael pauses reaching for his drink placed on the table. He takes a long drink before continuing. "There was this very loud crack of thunder she said. Then about a quarter of a mile from her base camp she explained it was like looking through a mirror." Michael explained with a weird relaxed look on his face. He again sits back in his chair and takes yet another drink of his scotch.

David just looks at Michael puzzled. "Looking through a mirror? What did she mean? What phenomena could possibly bring an event like this on? Did they do atmospheric or thermal activity checks of the area? What about seismograph activity?"

Robbie Thomas

Time Shift – The Paradigm

Michael takes another drag from his cigarette. "Yes, yes, yes!" Then he takes a drink from the scotch in his glass. "They did every check they possibly could think of. You know her. It's not like she would ever discount any opportunity to check and double check things, What is more surprising than any other event like this, is the fact they were able to...well, she called it like looking through the mirror effect."

David looks seriously at Michael, for what he has just heard has him baffled. "What's this mirror effect you keep taking about? What is it?"

Michael looks around the room then leans forward looking Professor Gates directly in the eye. "Shit David. They saw things that were horrendous, something we, us, the world are not ready for. What she described was something no man on earth has ever encountered before and damn if I am just going to sit back in some stuffy frigging classroom while all this passes us by!"

David picks up the newspaper one more time from the table in front of him as silence filled the room. "Michael, you're going to make me order another damn drink here. What are you saying? This sounds like a freaking sci-fi movie you're telling me. What in the world can or could produce something of a mirror effect? It's not feasible. Is it?"

Michael takes a huge swig of what was left in his glass, shakes the ice looking for more as he glances around the room for the waitress. "Well, you better order up pal! It's worse than that. This could be the fucking big break you been waiting for brother." Michael once again catches the eye of the waitress waiving to her ordering of another round of drinks while continuing to talk with David. "What they seen is not imaginable to mankind. They saw the other side of what would be

Robbie Thomas

considered the end of us. This is no damn science fiction movie. This is something unimaginable to you, or me and we are not going to miss out in this opportunity to discover it!"

David with a slight smirk on his face blurts out in a disbelief manner. "What?! What the hell are they smoking in that frigging jungle? You know, I have always said Elizabeth spends far too much time in the heat, especially in Peru. You expect me to just think the world is falling apart with this, this loud crack of thunder. The center of the earth, or some other dimension was breaking through. Come on Michael, get a grip!"

Michael looks very seriously at David, and then pulls out an envelope with a photograph in it. He hands it to David. "This is what she sent me through email. I printed it off but you can still make out everything. This is what one of them was able to catch with their cameras set up at base camp. You tell me what you see pal!"

David pulls the photo out of the envelope and looks at it. "Michael do you know what this means? This is incredible; we have to show this to the White House. The president has known about this. This has never happened as far as I know."

Michael sits back in his chair with a slight laugh under his breath. "They already know Dave. Things are being activated. Shit, they have implemented the Solarise Project while key marking all the data already." Michael takes a long drink of his scotch, wipes his mouth as he swallows the stiff gulp. "David, they want us to be in Peru by morning. The President is officially going to address this with his entire staff if he hasn't already. We were chosen to head a special scientific group going to Peru. So drink up my man, your famous!"

Robbie Thomas

Time Shift – The Paradigm

David stands up looks at Michael and can't believe what he is hearing. He grabs his brief case pauses before speaking. "Oh my god! I have to get home to Maggie. She is going to be pissed. You know how she is about surprises." David grabs his jacket from the opposite chair in front of him. "She is going to be so pissed at this. I'll catch up with you later, call me in an hour. Call me in one hour Michael!"

Michael raises his drink to David. "I know you David; you're always looking for that next big project. Here we go brother, cheers!" Then he takes a drink from his glass.

David picks up the photo again and stares at it while answering Michael. "Yah, Cheers! Project huh! I hope you know what we're getting ourselves into here Michael. I just hope we know."

Honey, I'm Home!

David walks into his house with the news of what Michael has just told him over drinks. He walks over to Maggie in the Kitchen while she is preparing dinner kissing her on the cheek, then begins to slowly break the news. You could hear a pin drop. The air has now changed with the anxious Professor trying to find the right words to tell his wife.

"Maggie, honey, you're not going to believe this. Now give me a minute to explain before you say anything. Michael just told me news of something that has happened in Peru."

Maggie puts down the knife she was using to peel the potatoes for dinner, picks up the pot on the counter filled with water and places it on the stove. "Hey! You're home early. I wanted to surprise you with dinner tonight. Making your favorite baked chicken with garlic mashed potatoes."

David grabs Maggie's hands guiding her over to the kitchen table and sits her down. He paces in the kitchen looking for the right words to explain to her what has just happened.

"Maggie, something has come up and it's serious!"

Maggie keeps her composure smiling waiting to hear what David is trying to tell her. "David, what are you up to now? When it comes to you and Michael I can only imagine. What is it?"

David rolls up his sleeves on his shirt while he takes a seat at the table where Maggie is now curiously waiting for the news.

"Michael and I had a meeting. You're not going to believe-"

Robbie Thomas

Maggie grins as she interrupts David mid-sentence. "I can only imagine when you start speaking with a sentence starting with Michael in it. Something is up. Now out with it David, I have dinner to finish." Maggie sarcastically looks at David. "What are you two up to...huh!"

David shifts in his chair reaching for Maggie's hand. "No Maggie. Something happened with Elizabeth in Peru. The government has launched the Solarise Project. It's big Maggie, really big. They are pulling out all the stops this time assembling a scientific team."

Maggie pulls her hand away giggling, brushes her hair out of her face as she walks over to the sink area, picks up the knife to continue peeling potatoes for dinner. "Oh don't be silly David. You know how Michael is. There's always with conspiracies or some phenomena happening somewhere in the world. Then it ends up being nothing but speculation."

David keeps a very serious look on his face as he is more determined to explain to Maggie what really is going on. "This is different! Here look at this." David reaches into his briefcase pulling out the newspaper with the photograph Michael gave him. "This was sent to Michael from Elizabeth in Peru. This isn't just speculation Maggie, have a look."

David throws the newspaper on the counter, along with the photograph Michael gave him. Maggie reacts with caution as she starts to look at the newspaper and picture.

"David, what the-"

David interrupts his wife as he is now pacing in his kitchen thinking. "That's right! The President has ordered Michael along with me to be briefed on this. This happening, whatever this is, we are not too sure as of yet, but Michael and myself are to be in Peru by morning under orders from the White House."

Maggie can't believe what she is hearing. All she can do is just stare at David in disbelief. "You're kidding me right?! You're not thinking of going are you David-"

Maggie is interrupted by the phone ringing. David answers it. "Hello?" It's the White House on the other end. David is totally taken back as he is immediately put through to the office of the President of the United States. He motions for Maggie to come listen to the conversation about to happen on the phone.

"Mr. Gates, my name is Martin Wedeman. I am the White House Secretary to the President of the United States. I trust you have been informed of what we have asked of you and your colleague?"

David looks at Maggie motioning to her intensely to come to the phone to listen to what is being told to him. "Yes, this is Professor Gates and yes I was told by my colleague some of what is going on."

The tension has now anxiously got both David and Maggie's attention. "The President has asked me to inform you, he would like to meet with you and Professor Wright this evening."

As David is speaking to the Secretary to the President on the phone, the doorbell rings. David and Maggie look at each other. David walks over to the door while still speaking to the White House as he peers out the little sheer on the front door. Mr. Wedeman starts to explain about the arrangements made for David.

Robbie Thomas

"That's ok Mr. Gates. Everything has been taken care of. In the next few minutes there are going to be some men who will show up at your home. Please don't be alarmed, they are there to escort you safely to the airport. There is a private plane waiting for you and your colleague to board. You will be flown immediately to Washington where you will then be brought to the White House to meet with the President of the United States."

David opens the door slowly. Several men in black with several dark SUV's parked out front of his house are now staring at him. "Mr. Wedeman. I think my ride is here!"

Mr. Wedeman responds to David's remark. "Good! The President is looking forward to meeting you. Good-bye Mr. Gates."

David turns looking at Maggie as she hugs him. "Maggie, baby!"

Maggie also turns looking at David now. She soon turns to quickly walk upstairs and yells back at him. "I know. I'll start packing for you."

David closes the door slowly as the men in black are still staring at him. He walks fast to the kitchen to grab his brief case, putting the newspaper and photo back into it as he yells to Maggie. "Don't pack too many things Maggie; just pack enough for a few days."

Maggie walks back downstairs with a small bag for David; she explains to him what she has packed. "I only put in a couple pairs of pants, shirts and socks. Also your shaving things, toothbrush and toothpaste. David, what is going on here, are we all in danger?"

David stops for a moment and embraces Maggie to reassure her.

"Maggie, I don't think it's extremely problematic, or something we can't figure out. I'm pretty sure the President and his team have things under control."

Maggie puts her head on his chest as they hug each other. She still explains her feelings of not being sure with it all to David. "I don't know David. I mean, we have the freaking men in black standing on our front porch. That's not a sign of having things under control to me!"

David kisses Maggie on the forehead. Hugs her and tries again to assure her. "It's going to be fine, you'll see. Don't worry I am sure this is all formality. Now look at me. I'll go meet the President, see what he has to say and go to Peru. I will meet up with Elizabeth and once I am briefed on what is going on, I will call you. I am sure it's nothing really to worry about."

Maggie settles for the explanation. "Ok…I'll hold you to it."

David smiles and pulls Maggie tight hugging her. "You can hold me now and when I get back.

David is now walking out the front door and being escorted to one of the black SUV's awaiting. "Remember, I'll call once I am in Peru!"

Maggie looking worried stands at the opening of the front door. "Love You!"

David enters the SUV. He is greeted by a man sitting in the front seat. "Good evening Mr. Gates. My name is Special Agent Rhoads. I will be escorting you along with your colleague here to the airport, please make yourself comfortable." David is looking at his wife waving to him as they drive off.

David acknowledges Special Agent Rhoads and smiles at Michael sitting on the other side of the SUV back seat. "Nice to meet you Agent Rhoads. Hello

Michael, nice meeting you here. How long until we get to the airport?"

Agent Rhoads turns handing Professor Gates an envelope. "We arrive in twenty minutes. We are leaving from Fort Campbell air base. In the meantime, I have been instructed to give you two this from the President."

David and Michael are handed the Presidential sealed envelope from Agent Rhoads. They both settle back and begin to tear open the letters.

"Professor Gates and Wright,

I wish there was a better way to introduce myself and what lay ahead for our nation. There seems to be no time to waste, so I won't beat around the bush. You're quite aware of your colleague Elizabeth Ross, who is working in Peru researching the old ruins of the Mayans. She seemed to have come across some sort of phenomena happening, that is now jeopardizing the security of the United States and the world. I have along with my staff conducted priority meetings with other nations about this strange occurrence. We have come to a conclusion to assemble scientists who might know how to deal with this situation. It has become more alarming as it isn't just contained to Peru, but has also spread to other countries such as Russia, Asia and more. I know I don't have to spell it out for you, for I am sure you know what is ahead of you both. Gentlemen, we are standing at the precipice looking at something bigger than us all. God only knows and we are at a loss right now in how to deal with it. Your country is calling upon you, asking for your assistance in figuring out what we as a nation, as a human race, are up against. I along with my staff will brief you more once you arrive this evening at the White House."

Samuel G. Morgan

Robbie Thomas

President of the United States of America

Michael looks over at David. "This makes it official! Well David, we most certainly have our work cut out for us this time. I wonder if Elizabeth was able to obtain any more information on the occurrence.

David slowly puts his hand down from reading the letter from the President of the United States. He takes a deep breath, turns to Michael and says, "I think we have more than just that. I hope we know what we are getting ourselves into here Michael."

Michael pulls out another envelope from his briefcase to share with David. "I just got this in from Elizabeth. More photos. Check out what she wrote on the bottom of one of them, I think you're going to want to see it."

David grabs the envelope from Michael, he looks at him puzzled, and then he looks toward the front of the SUV where agent Rhoads is looking on. He begins to open the envelope pulling out a series of photographs. These are different than the previous he has seen with Michael. "What the hell is that?! It looks like... Michael tell me I am not looking at something that resembles another place, or life form of some sort!" David continues to look at the photographs noticing what Elizabeth has written on the bottom of one of them. "She says, it is like looking through a hologram. A hologram? Do you know what this means?"

Michael raises his eyebrow looking at all in the SUV. "Indeed! If this is what I think it is, we are about to make history. Something like this has never occurred in our lifetime, or any lifetime for that matter. There has never been anything recorded in any document regarding any such phenomena. David, this is a first!"

David glances out the window of the SUV and collects his thoughts. A feeling of seriousness has just overwhelmed every fiber of his being. He begins to reflect to Maggie and the love he has for her. Trying to gather every wit about him to bring forward some sort of rational thought of what is going on. "Agent Rhoads, are you married? I don't mean to pry-"

Agent Rhoads looks back at David, noticing the seriousness on his face and replies. "Yes, and I have three children. Why do you ask?"

David looks with a pause at the Agent. "Don't you wish at times things were different? I mean for everyone in the world. No more famine, wars, sickness. Just a real simple life."

Agent Rhoads thinks for a brief moment. "Life would be really simplistic then wouldn't it?" He looks at David, "It would be worth waking up to everyday that's for sure!"

David finally got a deep feeling of knowing this was the very essence for the existence of man. He smiles as he slowly turns again to look out the SUV mumbling to himself. "I guess so. I guess you're right."

They arrive at the airbase where a private plane is waiting. The flight was a quick one as now they are arriving at the White House gates. The President is in high classified meeting with his staff regarding the situation around the world. They are preparing for the meeting with two of the country's top Scientists, Professor Gates and Professor Wright.

Secretary of State Robert Sims is briefing the President on the latest to come from NASA data. "Mr. President, the latest from NASA. This is what they have been able to pull off from their satellite about Peru."

The President's Personal Secretary interrupts to explain, that both Gates and Wright are on their way. "Excuse me Mr. President, the arrival has been confirmed. Your visitors are on route."

President Morgan looks up from his desk and nods saying, "Thank You Mr. Wedeman. Let me know as soon as they're here, will you please." He turns his attention to other important matters. "Robert, you know the Russians and even the Chinese are going to think this is something we have manipulated, either by using HAARP or the Solarise Project."

Secretary of State Robert Sims is looking over notes and data from NASA.

"With all due respect Mr. President, the Russians as well as the Chinese couldn't possibly put their data together to come up with a conclusion of this phenomenon." Robert looks through all the paperwork he has then shakes his head.

Vice President Donald Reece speaks up as he approaches the President's desk.

"Mr. President. We can't allow them to get there disrupting our operations at hand, especially now that we have our Air Craft Carrier the Roosevelt along with her destroyers off the coast."

President Morgan keeps a firm stance as he looks at both men. He collects his thoughts then explains. "Robert, Don. Let's not get too far ahead of ourselves here. There are many things happening around the world in every area. I am sure the Russians and the Chinese have their own problems. According to NASA data, the world seems to be in a heap of a mess here." The President points to all the data on his desk while picking up many reports indicating to those in the room, everyone has their problems at hand.

Secretary of State Robert Sims speaks up. "Mr. President, you now as well as I do, the Russians or the Chinese are going to blame-"

President Morgan quickly stands up from his desk and in a calming strong voice looks at Robert. "Hey, look! Both the Russians and the Chinese have had similar happenings in their countries. The CIA briefed me earlier. President Konstantine called me personally just hours ago expressing his thoughts on what is going on in his country. I don't expect some surprise attack from either the Chinese or the Russians. Let's let's not lose control of the situation, shall we." The President tosses the reports from his hands unto his desk looking at Robert Sims.

Robert agrees with the President. "Yes sir. I will notify General Saunders to send his report as soon as he makes contact."

Secretary of State Robert Sims leaves the Oval Office to notify the General that the President is waiting on his report. The President gets up from his chair, walks over to the Oval Office window and just stares outside. "God help us all!"

Meanwhile in Russia, the Russians High Command is in a high level alert meeting. They are deploying their army to the affected areas as destruction is beginning in the far east of Russian territory. A complete city has fallen victim to the phenomena as buildings are destroyed. People are dead throughout the town and the landscape is totally changed. The door of death has opened; it seems to be swallowing up the living leaving the echoes of cries for help from those who once lived there.

Robbie Thomas

Time Shift – The Paradigm

General of the Russian Army Alexei Potinov briefs President Konstantine of the activity and deployment of his troops. "Mr. President. We have deployed the first, second and seventh armoured divisions to the region of Domensk. Colonel Remink will report shortly as to what he engaging in the region. The preliminary reports suggest there is some loss of life in the region, while others have very little if any loss at all."

President Konstantine looks at the General with worry on his face as he gathers his thoughts. "Good! I want to know immediately his further findings. Have him report to my office as soon as he arrives. I also want a team of medical personal on the ground assisting the villages in the area as soon as possible."

General Potinov starts to walk out of the President's office then stops. He slowly turns back with a puzzled look on his face."Yes Sir, Mr. President. Mr. President do you think the Americans are going to see this as an act of aggression on our own people, or a tactic to involve them in some type of engagement?"

President Konstantine sits at his desk looking at the preliminary report. He removes his glasses sets them down on the desk, rubs his eyes looking around the room at General Potinov. "Don't be silly Alexei. The Americans may be a little slow, somewhat not as sophisticated as they think they are, but they are not looking at us right now. They are more concerned at present with Peru and their archaeological finds."

Igor Vladimir is the Prime Minister of Defense for Russia. He sits very quiet in a chair listening to the conversations between President Konstantin and General Potinov and then remarks. "With Peru? Why on earth Peru? Are they digging up the

Robbie Thomas

Time Shift – The Paradigm

past to fix the future? What do these Americans seem to think they can do by

digging up such things?"

President Nicolas Konstantin turns in his chair, looks out his office window

while he speaks to the Prime Minister about the Americans. "It seems they have a

small group of scientists digging up relics and now they are sending more people to

the area. They are digging up the past, to figure out the future. Digging up the past to

figure out the future."

Unrest in Country

As news spreads quickly throughout the world of all the tragic happenings in various countries, back home in small farming community of Owensville Kansas, news of the United States falling siege to a Paranormal Phenomenon is just unheard of as well as unthinkable. Owensville Kansas is not even listed on many maps whatsoever, yet it is this little out of the way place with a small population where everyone knows everyone. This quiet little community is about to fall victim of something much more than a coincidental encounter and not by choice. Circumstances are vastly arising that seem to shut this community off from the rest of the world. The people of Owensville are in a panic mode shuffling about wanting to know more from the towns Sherriff by holding a town hall meeting. They hope to find out more of what is going on with the United States and the rest of the world.

The small grocery store on Main Street seems to be the go to place as the Mayor is the actual owner of the store and at the moment it's the only place where any reception of telecommunications is possible. Many of the town's council, Sherriff along with some concerned towns folks gather to see the news on the only television that is working in the entire area. The uptown area is very busy with the rest of the towns people purchasing supplies from the hardware store, gas station while rushing around to gather whatever they can as fear has now encompassed everyone in this tiny farming community.

Sheriff Dale Higgins has his Deputy on the outskirts of town observing what seems to be huge movement by the United States Military a few miles from town. Deputy Travis Parker has been radioing back and forth updates to the Sheriff and keeping him updated to what is going on with the Military movements. Things for the most part are completely out of the ordinary for this community. Those who are keeping a cool head about things are feeling the pinch of something much bigger is happening concerning their town, which has the Sheriff analyzing everything.

The grocery story is very busy with many shouting, asking questions, wanting to know what is going on. Frustrations are setting in fast with fear of an apocalypse on everyone's mind. Pandemonium has set in as the Sheriff is at the end of his rope with all the havoc going on in the once quiet little town and he wants to restore order.

Higgins tries to quiet the people who have gathered in the grocery store seeking answers of the tragedy going on around the United States.

"People, people, quiet please. Will everyone just shut up for a minute?" Having a hard time convincing the mass gathered he pulls out his sidearm and shoots off one round into the ceiling of the grocery story. Everyone comes to a quick stop looking at the Sheriff. "Sorry I had to do that, but you people have to listen to me. Let's keep it sane in here, can we do that?!"

Mayor Charlie Doyle looks at what the Sheriff has just done to his grocery store ceiling and is totally surprised at his actions. "Dale, that is so going to cost you!"

"Yah, yah! Send me the bill Charlie." Higgins has now gotten everyone's attention and wants to inform them of the latest news from Parker. "I'm sorry I had to do that folks, but you have to give me a minute to talk here. Now I have Parker on the outskirts of town watching what is going on a few miles from here. The military have and are setting up some type of perimeter around Owensville-."

The town's folk once again start up the loud chatter in the grocery store wanting to know what it is the military wants from them. The chaos of everyone pushing and shoving, talking all at once at the Sheriff, is making matters worse now. Higgins looks to Charlie signaling to have the lights turned off. Once the lights are turned off, everyone once again quiets down as they're caught off guard with going dark.

Higgins once again addresses everyone in the store asking them to settle down while he explains. "Now look here everyone! If you want to hear what is going on, then I suggest you keep it quiet for a minute. Give me a chance to explain, is that clear?" The store becomes quiet as one of the towns folk, Sal Dickens speaks up asking a question.

"What are we going to do Sheriff? Where are we going to go? Sal moves up from the back of the room towards the front of the store where the Sheriff is standing on a chair addressing everyone. "What do you propose we all do Dale? There's nowhere to go because the military has us cut off from the rest of the world-".

The crowd rumbles on after the last statement Sal Dickens has made. The Sheriff once again raises his hands and shouts out to everyone.

"People look, shut up will you! Now Sal, I know you mean well and bless that beautiful wife of yours for putting up with you all these years, but at this very moment we are all going to settle our heads down. Go collect your families together letting them know to calm down. We are working on this problem and I will have more information for everyone once I find out what it is the Military wants from us.

Now I suggest everyone go home, there isn't anything anyone can do by running

around in the streets buying up everything causing havoc and putting fear into

everyone in town. I will be back here at six o'clock this evening to update those who

wish to come, but if I have anyone of you making a ruckus again like you did today,

you won't be let in the store. Is that clear?"

The crowd quietly mumbles to each other in a low tone as it seems the

Sheriff has gotten through to them. The towns folk slowly start to disperse exiting

the store as finally order for the time being has been established by the Sheriff.

Mayor Doyle watches everyone leaving the store, and then turns to the

Sheriff wanting to know more. "Well Dale, you sure got your work cut out for you.

What do you propose we do now?" Doyle walks over to the front doors of the

grocery store locking them. "You know they are all going to be back here at six

wanting to know what it is you have for them. What are you going to do now Dale?"

"You know Charlie, as long as you have known me, have I ever let you

down before?" Higgins just stands at the front doors looking at all the people

running about in the streets in fear. "But you know, this time I have no idea what the

hell we are up against. I have no idea why the military has parked themselves

outside of town, but I am sure going to find out."

On the outskirts of town, the ongoing military buildup is keeping Deputy

Parker busy watching from his squad car parked behind a big old Oak Tree. Deputy

Parker thinks he is being evasive by trying to hide behind the tree and brush that

surrounds the area, however, the military already know he is there harmlessly watching them set up. Huge military convoys of equipment are arriving by the minute with satellite dishes and many military personnel. Helicopters are flying about on the perimeter of the town while the commotion on the ground is quickly escalating.

"Parker, what's going on now? Parker are you there?" Sheriff Higgins is trying to get a hold of Deputy Parker to find out what if anything has changed in the last hour. "Parker are you there? Come in, over."

Parker hears the Sheriff calling for him as he is standing by the Oak Tree looking through his binoculars. He runs back to the squad car to answer back. "Yes Sheriff. Sheriff you should see this. They got many transport trucks coming in with satellites on them, helicopters flying about the area and many soldiers on the ground."

"What do you make of it Travis?" The Sheriff is in his car driving over to his house watching everyone in town still running about.

"To me Sheriff, I think they are setting up a perimeter to cut us all off from leaving town, or anything from coming into town. I don't understand Sheriff. Its like they are quarantining us." Deputy Parker notices something, puts the radio down and gets out of the squad car to take a look. "Sheriff, I think you better get over here."

"I'll be up there in about twenty minutes. I am going to stop by Molly and the kids to make sure they're ok first. Just keep an eye and don't get too close."

The Sheriff is now making his way up the long drive to his house to check on his family. Off in the distance he can see the helicopters flying about when something really strange starts to occur. He stops his car, looks real hard, but can't

Robbie Thomas

make out what it is. He finally makes it to his house where his wife Molly comes running out of the house to meet him.

"Dale, what on earth is going on?" Molly hugs Dale as he then bends down to pick up his youngest son. "Dale what's with all those helicopters flying around outside of town?"

"I don't know Molly, but Travis is up on the ridge keeping an eye on them. It seems they are also bringing in large equipment setting it all up a couple miles from town." The Sheriff puts his youngest son down on the ground to go play. "Molly I want you to pack up a few things. Keep it very light, only things we need as essentials. Where's Jessica?"

Molly looks really worried now that the Sheriff has told her to pack. "Why do we need to pack? What's going on? We don't have television it's still out, no radio either. Dale, I'm scared!"

Dale hugs his wife, assuring her. "Molly there are things happening around the world more so than what we know of since the last news broadcast we've seen. Since the television has gone off things have escalated. Now what concerns me is this, why is the military closing off Owensville-?"

Jessica, who just turned sixteen, comes out of the house while Molly and Dale walk up the steps. "Dad, what's happening?"

The Sheriff walks over and kisses Jessica on the forehead and gives her a hug. "I don't know baby, but I want you and mom to pack a few things, ok? We're going to go on a little trip." He turns to look where his son is yelling out to him. "Payton, come give dad a hand, will you?!"

Robbie Thomas

"Dale, we need to call mother and tell her too." Molly walks over to the phone to call her mother. "You know she is sitting there worried for us. She is going to want us to go there."

Dale is listening to what Molly is saying to him as she picks up the phone to call her mother. He is standing by the kitchen sink looking out the window in the direction the phenomena is happing. For the most part, it's changing and taking shape. It has gone from a total blur, to something resembling looking through a mirror. He doesn't like what he is seeing and knows that Deputy Parker is waiting for him on the ridge.

Dale walks over to Molly who is on the phone to her mother. "I need to head up to the ridge where Travis is. I won't be long, promise" He grabs his keys he put down on the counter top and begins to walk out the door just off the kitchen.

"Wait!" Molly yells out to Dale. "Just a minute mom. Dale is leaving again." Molly holds the phone to her chest looking at her husband. "You be careful please. I love you!"

Dale holding the door looks at his son and then to Molly. "I love you too. Don't worry, I won't be long. We'll be on the road to your mom's as soon as I get back." He walks out the door and back to his car and grabs the radio. "Travis, I'm on my way."

Higgins drives off looking at both directions seeing the commotion with the helicopters and the phenomena happening in the opposite direction. There is a loud crack of thunder, something that has never been heard before, not even in one of the worst storms the area has ever had. The Sheriff pulls his car to a screeching stop, looking in his rear view mirror noticing a change in the phenomena behind him. The eerie strange configuration that is taking place on the opposite side of town is now growing in proportions, which could just engulf the town of Owensville. He steps on the gas and speeds off in the direction where Deputy Parker is waiting.

Meanwhile, in town, Doyle and some of his councilmen have closed off all roads leading in the direction of the Phenomena. People in the town are now in high panic mode from the loud crack of thunder and the change that is taking place. People are in high gear grabbing anything they can as supplies, while others are boarding up their homes in fear of the event happening. The Streets are now becoming very empty as the last of the residents are leaving heading home. It has now become a ghost town with no activity whatsoever.

The Sheriff finally arrives where Deputy Parker is watching the movement by the military. He gets out of his vehicle and walks up the small ridge to the top, where the Oak Tree offers little cover for them to spy on the goings on of the military buildup.

"Hey! So what's going on Travis?"

"You should see this. It's just nuts what they are doing. Look for yourself." Deputy Parker hands the Sheriff the binoculars as he has a peak into what it is the military are up to. "You see those big rigs with the huge satellite radar things, they been up and running now for the last half hour. There is a huge army of men coming in many trucks as well. . I don't like this!"

Higgins is noticing everything the Deputy is saying as he looks over everything that's going on. "I hear you Travis. There seems to be something the military knows and we are sitting right smack in the middle of it all."

Travis looks in the opposite direction to the event unfolding behind them. "You don't think what that thing is… had anything to do with the earthquake in California do you-.

Just as the deputy asks the Sheriff about the event, they are met with a platoon of soldiers in complete hazard suits and masks pointing guns at them. This caught both the Sheriff and the Deputy off guard.

"You have to get off this ridge and back to town. You are not permitted to be here. Please evacuate this area as it is now off limits to you and the town's people!" One of the soldiers explains to both Higgins and Parker. "You are ordered away from this region immediately!"

"Excuse me boy! You don't own this land and we are the law around here am I making myself clear" Parker speaks up and is a bit irate at what is going on. "I think soldier boy here-'

"If you don't remove yourself from this ridge immediately we will be forced to detain you. Sheriff Higgins and Deputy Parker we ask that you cooperate with us. Go back to town. You can be more useful keeping law and order with the people there." The one solder hands the Sheriff a small package. "In here, are instructions you must follow. Take this back to town, read it over then act on it."

"How do you know who we are? Who the hell are you guys?!" Parker is getting upset.

Higgins looks at the package he is handed which have been handed him from the one soldier. "It's ok Travis; let's do what they ask of us. Ok soldier, we will

Robbie Thomas

leave we don't want to have any problems here at all." The Sheriff and the Deputy both get into their vehicles and drive off back toward town.

While the Sheriff is driving off, he looks one more time back at the soldiers standing there watching the two drive back to town. Thoughts of being imprisoned run through his mind as on one side of town this phenomena has them trapped and on the other side is the United States Military quarantining them. He now has to head back to the grocery store to inform the Mayor and others what he has found out. He looks down at the package handed to him by the soldier that sits on his front seat wondering its contents. As Higgins and Parker pull up to the front of the grocery store they are met with the town's Mayor.

"Dale, did you hear that crack of thunder-." The Mayor is quickly interrupted and pulled into his grocery store by Sheriff Higgins. "What's going on Dale? You look like you've seen a ghost!"

"Charlie, there's more going on up on the ridge than we know!" Higgins walks over to the windows of the grocery store looking outside seeing if any of the townsfolk are coming to the store. He wants to break the news to the Mayor before anyone arrives. "The Army are conducting some type of exercise. They intercepted Travis and me handing me this package. They ordered us back to town-."

Parker quickly speaks up. "Not only that, but they have blocked the only way into town with many soldiers and equipment."

"Why on earth would they do this? Didn't you tell them you're the law around here?!" The Mayor takes the package the Sheriff is handing him. "What's this?"

"Open it up Charlie. I think it's telling us we are quarantined. They have the entire area completely in lock down. No way in and no way out!" Sheriff Higgins walks over to the telephone in the store to call his wife. "Charlie I would post signs in your windows telling everyone about this, so it saves time explaining to each person coming in here."

The phone rings back at the Sheriff's home as Molly picks up.

"Hello?"

"Hey Molly it's me. Look, call your mom back telling her I think we will be a bit late."

"Why? What's wrong Dale?"

"It seems the military has the roads all blocked off. They won't let anyone in or out of the town."

"You're kidding right. You're the Sheriff! Can't you make them move?"

"I wish it were that easy, Molly. They have quarantined the entire town and area. They ordered me and Travis off the ridge and they didn't have squirt guns in their hands." The Sheriff notices some of the people are returning to the grocery store to hear what he has to say, it's now five minutes to six in the evening. "Molly, I have to let you go. I have to let people from the town know what's going on."

"I will see you soon. Love you, Dale."

"Love you too, babe. I'll see you once I'm done here. Bye for now." Higgins hangs up as he watches the store start to fill up of town's folk.

"Travis, can you post these on the windows for me? Thank you." The Mayor hands Parker a few signs he printed off asking folks to stay in their homes until

Time Shift – The Paradigm

further notice.

Sheriff Higgins comes out of the office after speaking with Molly on the phone. "Ok Charlie, I think we better let everyone know what's going on." The Sheriff moves to the front of the store. "Ok folks, can I have your attention please. Deputy Parker and I met with some of the military today to which they have instructed us to tell you all to remain calm. They want everyone to know they are here to help us and therefore we are to remain in our homes until further notice."

Sal Dickens, the towns' outspoken one, speaks up again addressing the issue at hand. "So what you're saying is that we're all prisoners here in this town until good old Uncle Sam says different? Is that what your trying to tell us Sheriff?"

"No Sal, I'm not saying that at all. What I want to say, if you give me a chance, is that the military is doing an exercise a couple miles out of town and the access is temporarily cut off from the north coming or going into town."

The crowd starts again to get loud and a bit anxious because of what the Sheriff has just told them. They all start to ask questions at the same time, which is making it a bit noisy in the grocery store.

The Sheriff puts his hands in the air to signal everyone to listen to him. "Quiet please! Just a minute everyone. They told us to return to town to tell all of you to remain calm. So for now, can all of you just go back home to your families, have dinner or whatever it is that you do. I am sure this will all pass very soon."

"Ok everyone you heard the Sheriff! Let's go people. I am sure you have better things to do than hang around here. Come on Sal, let's get you home to your wife." Deputy Parker escorts Sal Dickens to the door.

Robbie Thomas

"Yep! I can see who isn't going to be Sheriff once we get that other one out of office. You know Travis, I use to like you but you're too much like that other pretend cop over there." Sal pulls his arm away from Deputy Parker looking back at the Sheriff. "Yep! Too much like him you are."

"Well I will take that as a compliment coming from you Sal. Now don't keep your lovely wife waiting any longer. You know how she gets if you been out a spell!" Deputy Parker closes the door and locks it just after Sal Dickens leaves the store. "I thought he would never leave. There's something seriously wrong with that guy" Deputy Parker mumbles to himself.

"Travis! Come here for a sec," The Sheriff wants to discuss an initiative to keep the towns folk calm. "The three of us have to come up with a plan. Now we know how certain individuals, like Sal for instance, will want to cause trouble-".

"You're not kidding. Man that guy is a pain in the ass at times!" Deputy Parker remarks.

"We have to keep law and order for the for the most part. I am not afraid to put Sal or anyone in jail for the night if that has to be the case." Higgins stresses. "If we can, let's try to keep everyone calm until we know what is going on with the military. I have no idea what the hell that thing is that's on the south side of town, but we're sure going to find out."

"I don't know Dale, but I hope it's nothing that is going to cause harm to anyone." The Mayor is very concerned of the happenings taking place around his town of Owensville. "I sure hope you and the military know what you're doing. I have a real bad feeling about this."

Robbie Thomas

The three men agree and are staring out the front window in the direction of the phenomena that is happening to the south. The paranormal phenomenon not only has the attention of the military and the small town of Owensville Kansas, but the entire world is experiencing something that is not fathomable by mankind. The sleepy little town has now become the center focus of a mystery that is plaguing the world.

Time Shift – The Paradigm

Meeting the President

Both Professor Gates and Wright are met by White House Chief of Staff

Anne Reynolds. They are quickly escorted through the White House Halls being

briefed on what is going on throughout Peru. She explains what the President

expects from them giving both men some details before they enter the Oval Office.

"Hello Mr. Gates and Mr. Wright, nice to meet both of you. I trust your

travel was pleasant. Now we don't have much time gentlemen, so if you so kindly

could follow me the President is waiting."

Michael shakes Anne Reynolds hand thanking her for the reception. "Nice to

meet you as well, Ms. Reynolds. As pleasant as one could expect given the

circumstances."

David also extends his hand acknowledging Anne Reynolds. "Pleasure is all

mine. Like Michael says, we wish it was under different circumstances,

nevertheless, we will accommodate the President anyway we can."

Anne Reynolds looks at both Professors smiles handing them each a briefing

package. "Well, this is for you. Both the contents of this portfolio, as well as what I

am about to tell you, plus whatever the President says, remains with you. We do not

need a panic on our hands. Understood?"

David looks at Michael then back to Anne. "Absolutely! Everything is and will

remain mum."

Anne Reynolds looks at Michael with seriousness. "Mum? Mr. Gates, if any

of this gets out to the general public, even to your lovely wife Maggie, could you

imagine the amount of panic this can cause? Mum? I would consider my mouth

Robbie Thomas

remains shut. Yes, that is the word I would use."

"Not a word Ms. Reynolds. Not a word, right David?" Michael cordially responds for David.

David totally agrees. "Absolutely not a word."

Anne Reynolds smiles then abruptly stops regaining the composure of the situation. "Good. Glad we have this understanding. Follow me would you please gentlemen. The President is expecting you."

The three are now walking down the West Wing Hall of the White House towards the Oval office. Secret Service agents that are posted along the way continue to radio ahead notifying the progression of Mr. Gates and Mr. Wright as they are escorted through the historical hallway. Michael and David are amazed at all the art work, architecture as well as security there is in the White House. While the White House Chief Of Staff walks with the two professors, she explains what is going on as they near the door to the Oval Office of the President.

"Ok, what we know so far is that there were a series of time shifts, sort of an earth dementia happening in Peru, England, Russia and China. These are our preliminary reports for now, however, we assume there is much more going on. That is where the both of you come in."

David frowns, listening to what the Secretary of State is saying while looking at Michael. "Time shifts and dementia? Are you suggesting a parallel extension of an opening to a window has occurred?"

Michael quickly reiterates a sense of being unsure as to what Anne has just explained. "That's literally impossible. Not impossible but not heard of and has never been proven. This is just a theory that has never been proven on any scale of the imagination. Do you know what you're saying Ms. Reynolds?"

The three come to a stop in front of the Oval Office door. They are about to enter the President's Office to meet the President of the United States along with his staff. Anne Reynolds stops, looks at both Professors pauses, then says one last thing before entering the office.

"Not impossible Professor nor is it impractical. It has happened. That is why you have been summoned to the President. I suggest gentlemen with all the knowledge you have and aspire to have; I would muster it up at this moment. Come up with some explanation as how to help fix this or we will all be history. I for one, love living my life in the now as I am sure both of you are as well. It's time to put all those years of teaching to the test Gentlemen. The nation, hell, the world is depending on it. Welcome to the White House and welcome to the President's Office!"

Anne Reynolds opens the door walking into the Oval Office where the President along with other high ranking members of his staff is waiting.

Anne introduces both Professors to the President of the United States. "Mr. President, Professors David Gates and Michael Wright."

The president is overlooking reports of the phenomena, which is holding the world captive. The mood in the Oval Office is one of very intense anxiety as the two professors enter it. There are many other high ranking officials conversing with the President on the situation trying to determine what the next move would be. The President raises his head peering over his glasses looking at Ms. Reynolds and the

Time Shift – The Paradigm

two Professors. President Morgan gets out of his chair walks around the Oval Office Desk to greet both Professors.

"Ah yes, come in gentlemen please. Very nice to meet both of you. I trust your trip here was pleasant. Thank You Ms. Reynolds. I trust Anne has given you both a short briefing on what is going on. Please won't you take a seat gentlemen?"

Both Michael and David shake the Presidents hand. Then both seat themselves in chairs opposite the Presidents chair at the Oval Office Desk. The excitement both men have is overwhelming as they are sitting in front of the commander and chief of the United States of America.

David speaks thanking the President. "Yes, thank you! It's very nice to meet you as well Mr. President."

Michael also thanks President Morgan. "Yes the trip was very uneventful. Mr. President this surely is a pleasure to meet you."

The President smiles then quickly turns to business at hand. "Gentlemen I guess the formalities are out of the way. I want to get down to business if you don't mind. What we have or let me put it this way, what the world has at this very moment is a crises like non other." President Morgan picks up some of the notes given him on his desk and begins to hand them over to both Professors. "Now Professors, I don't want you to sugar coat anything nor would I expect you to hold back any thoughts you might have. The very reason you are here today in my office is to be very direct and upfront. We know what is going on in certain areas of the world as well as in our own nation. What we don't know is, why and who or what is doing this. Now, there has been speculation it was the Russians and their new

Robbie Thomas

experiments they are undertaking with their own version of HAARP. That summation has been diminished by not only conversations with the President of Russia but by our own satellite images taken two days prior of the first anomaly."

David interjects a suggestion to the president. "Yes sir, she has explained something of an event which has occurred that might be of a dimensional happening. I was also thinking Mr. President if you allow me."

"By all means, please do." President Morgan encourages the professor.

David shifts himself forward in his chair and begins to explain. "I have this theory if you will, well not so much a theory but a probable. If the Mayans were right-"

David is quickly interrupted by Michael who really doesn't like where David is going with this conversation. "Sorry Mr. President, my colleague has good intentions; he really does but David, really, where do you think the Mayan-"

As quickly as Michael had interrupted, David reiterates what he was trying to say. "Mr. President, like I was saying before I was rudely interrupted. The Mayan predicted many different happenings throughout the centuries to which most, if not all come true. Now what is amazing about these predictions as you probably know, they all happened well after the existence of that culture that was written in stone so to speak."

President Morgan listens very intensely to what Professor Gates is saying. "Yes please continue!"

David takes a breath then again fixes his posture in the chair. "Well Sir, in many of my studies along with research, one particular notation made by the Mayan was the fact of a time shift. A time shift, which had a paradigm of different

dimensions, which would co-exist with our life as we know it."

President Morgan sits quietly with his eyes fixated on David. "Continue!"

"The Mayan were very spiritual people who pride themselves on revelations.

They were great scholars of the stars and of visions shown them. They would often

make writings set in stone literally to warn coming generations of pending doom.

There is a tablet one of my students often talks about that was part of an

archaeological dig several years back that contained such pending doom. Yet, and I

must say, there might be an outcome of what they had written in stone that has a

way out of such tragedy."

President Morgan takes a stern look at Professor Gates. "Please, I don't mean

any disrespect, continue. This is sounding like a block buster movie and I am very

interested in hearing the conclusion."

Michael has a small laugh at the expense of his colleague. The rest of the

room and staff members as well join in on the not so much believable situation

David is telling them. David struggles with what is going on in the room at the

moment but bears down deciding to continue to convince everyone and the President

of the United States.

"No really Sir, there was a tablet that explained exactly what we are going

through at this moment, but it did mention a different outcome. This is where it gets

a bit difficult to figure out!"

"Difficult to figure out?" The President looks around the room at his staff

then back to professor Gates. "David, please forgive me, but that is what we do. We try to figure out things, so let's cut to the chase shall we."

"Yes Sir! Well, part of the tablet is missing. The part that ended had as much information explaining our world as we know it. A transformation of sorts that had a pending doom was etched very clearly on it. Then out of the doom there was a different path that would or could lead to an outcome other than an end of us all."

President Morgan sits up in his chair now and leans forward onto his desk. "Professor, have you or have any of your colleagues figured out what they were trying to say?"

David looks again at Michael then back to the President. "No Sir, this is the missing link to the puzzle, were I a betting man, I'd wager they were telling us that there's a way out of this mess. It's up to all of us to figure that out!"

President Morgan sits very still looking around the room for a brief moment, taking in the information given him by David. "Well, that is where you come in professor Gates and Professor Wright. I want you to work for me now. I want you to go to Peru, find out what exactly did transpire. There is too much going on around the world at this time. Russia has had something occur; China has had something happen as well. Europe is all in a mess! We need answers and those answers have to be accurate and quick. Life as we know it depends on what you can do. We are running out of time gentlemen, we need a solution to this problem. If you're right about this Mayan prophecy Professor Gates, then you have the knowledge to better understand what we are up against, more so than my staff you see here in my office. The both of you will head up a team headed for Peru under my command and you report directly back to my office. Gentlemen, I don't have to tell you that every living being on this planet is at the mercy of this thing or this phenomena going on. What I will tell you is that every minute we waste not doing something about it will end us all for sure. I want you to go and figure this thing out making it stop, do we understand?"

Vice President Donald Reese walks into the Oval office with more information on what is going on around the world. "Excuse me Mr. President, the latest from Russia."

President Morgan looks at Donald Reese. "Thank you! Don, I like you to meet professor Gates and Wright. They are here to help us better understand what is going on right now with our world."

Donald Reese shakes the hands of both Professors. "Gentlemen, pleasure. I trust with the amount of knowledge and expertise you two have, you will be able to help sort this out for us."

Professor Gates and Wright both answer at the same time. Gates, "Yes Sir, sure going to try", Wright, "Absolutely, yes we will"

Donald Reese smiles back at the two men. "Good glad to hear it!"

The Vice President turns handing the President newly acquired information from the Russians. "Sam, the Russians are transmitting something about a complete city in the Domensk Region. It has been reduced to rubble. No life available, completely gone!"

This news about the Russian region has caught the attention of Michael as he eagerly wants to look at the report to give his thoughts. "Mr. President, may I?"

President Morgan quickly agrees. "By all means, that's why you're here.

Enlighten us won't you Please."

Michael stands up looking at the President and Mr. Reese. "Now I know this might sound a bit out of a science fiction book or movie, but if my theory is right, with what has been predicted by many prophets from thousands of years ago plus the physics behind this phenomenon-"

Donald Reese can't believe what he is hearing come from such an astute Professor who is standing in the Oval Office of the President. "You've got to be kidding me, Sam?!"

"Hear him out Donald, let's give them the opportunity to enlighten us., We might just might learn something. Hell, with everything going on in the world, listening to our own two highly respected scientists isn't going to hurt now is it?"

Donald Reese still can't believe what is going on in the President's Office. "But Sam, prophets? prediction? Come on. The world is in crises; surely we have no time for this fairy tale story."

The President sits back in his chair looking up at Donald Reece. He puts his hands together with his two index fingers over his lips thinking. Then he sits forward once more to speak to what Donald Reese just said. "Well Don, as long as I have known you, you have been the pillar upon which I trust. Now let's trust them for me and hear them out. We can give the respect that is needed in a professional way to our guests. Now give them the opportunity to explain to us all."

The President once again looks at both professors. "Gentlemen, Please continue."

Michael looks at Mr. Reese who is listening now very intensely wanting to know where this is all going to lead. " The Mayan have predicted thousands of years ago of a turn in mankind, this is where Professor Gates can explain more being that he is the historian as I am the Physicist. If my theory is right, the implications of a dimensional shift would mean the two worlds, our world here and another force or let's say realm co existent to us is being forced together through time and space."

President Morgan is now very interested in what Michael and David have been trying to explain to him and his staff. "So, what your trying to say is, when two side by side co existing worlds collide or try to occupy that same space, it could mean a dimensional shake up. Is that what you mean?"

Michael corrects the President in his assumption. "It wouldn't be a dimensional shake up Mr. President. It would be the annihilation of life as we know it here on earth!"

The President is now really thinking hard on what he has just been told then turns to David Gates asking, "Professor Gates, can you add to this?"

"Sir, the Mayan calendar has predicted the end of times for thousands of years. The accuracy of their predictions are very notable. Predictions from other groups such as the Hopi Indians, the writing on the walls in the Pyramids in Egypt all point to the same thing.

Donald Reese once again interrupts the conversation between the two professors and the President. "Alright, just take what has been given and let's just say your one hundred percent right. What are the chances of reversing this devastation and who do you assume could do this. I'm just hypothetically thinking here."

President Morgan smiles as he watches his Vice President is on the objective side of things. "Gentlemen you're going to have to excuse my esteemed colleague, somehow this over the top assumption, now no disrespect to your work but I think it has him at a disadvantage. When I picked Mr. Reese to be my running mate, I knew I had the best of the best to which this office has never seen before. As you see in his method of questioning your accountability of what is your thoughts on this matter, he has most certainly shown why he my Vice President and a damn good one at that. Now Professor Gates please continue, we should bring this meeting to a close."

"It is very plausible and the reality of it is, the predictions from many cultures have come true that have aligned themselves to other historical events. We can't just disregard the inevitable or what has been written Mr. President, for its happening now!"

The President sits back in his chair at the Oval Office Desk and pauses for a brief moment to collect his thoughts while looking at everyone in the room. The only noise you can hear is the ticking of the clock on the President's desk. It seems as though minutes upon minutes are going by as the President is in deep thought. As the President looks to each individual in the room he is justifying his thoughts to which he is going to speak making a command to his staff.

"Anne, I want these two on a plane right away for Peru. Sam, I want them to have everything we can offer them in assistance so whatever they need make sure they get it. Also Don, your still my pillar just now I want you to trust me on this one. Ok people, we don't have much more time to lose; we have to move on this and move now. The people of the United States are depending on us, the people of the world are too. Move people!"

The office of the President is now alive with the hustle of paper work being collected by his staff. The rush of a new precipitated anxiety is filling the room as finally there are orders handed down from the commander and chief. President Morgan, walks around his desk puts his hands on the shoulders of the two Professors looking them in the eyes.

"You know gentlemen; many historical decisions have been made from this office. Many great men have sat at this desk to make those decisions. Today we all sit at this desk making a historical decision for mankind; we don't want to let them down. God Bless America and God Bless Mankind!

Polar Melt Down

Wednesday: 06:00 hours, somewhere near the North Pole. A European team

of scientists lead by Dr. Alan Hendricks, the founding father of the theory that time

in space revolves around vibration and sound, are conducting experiments at station

Zebra. For the last two years data collecting of vital information has been

systematically logged to corroborate the fact the North Pole is most certainly

melting, however, melting while shifting at an alarming rate. The team consists of a

total of six scientists, which each are experts in their own fields.

The Chardon Corporation, that funds the expedition along with all the

experiments, are in high level meetings with their CEO's and management regarding

the happenings going on around the world. The latest data submitted by Dr.

Hendricks suggests there has been a more substantial movement, but on a different

level. There have been readings recorded pointing to something other than the Polar

Cap moving. There is an element of different data that has been measured, which

has the scientists baffled. Temperatures and atmospheric pressure gages seem to

fluctuate at a radical pace that doesn't quite measure up to what is the normal in any

aspect. The emergency meetings for the most part are being met with apprehension

while decisions regarding the project at hand are getting mixed reviews.

Some of the top management would like to see the expedition pulled, as

unexpected phenomena revolving around the Polar Cap is starting to hinder the

original project. The investment regarding the outlook for Dr. Hendricks'

experiments is in question as the Chardon Corporation would like to stop the entire

project. The very thought of something dangerous or an unknown anomaly

Robbie Thomas

occurring doesn't sit well with investors and now the pressure is on the corporation to act immediately to save stock values. Radio contact in the last month or so has been very infrequent therefore; notifying the scientist for anything has been very diminishing at best. Time is running out as the Paranormal Phenomena is increasingly growing by the hour leaving Station Zebra very vulnerable as well as their occupants.

As a rare storm is approaching Station Zebra, the scientists are expecting two corporate representatives to arrive by plane to observe while they hand Dr. Hendricks the bad news of the termination of the project. Everyone on the project is not expecting the news, as they all prepare for their visitors to arrive. The plane is approaching the Station and about to land where a welcoming party is waiting to take the visitors to the main building. The plane lands without any problems and the two corporate representatives are now greeted by Dr. Jun Aurora from Japan and Dr. Leon Petit from France. Dr. Aurora and Dr. Petit are the first to greet David Lynch along with Nathan Giles, who have spent the last twelve hours flying in from the United Kingdom.

Dr. Aurora offers his hand in welcoming the two gentlemen. "Hello! Welcome gentlemen. Trust your flight was without incident." Dr. Aurora shakes both men's hands introducing Dr. Leon Petit. "I am Dr. Jun Aurora and this is Dr. Leon Petit. He is in charge of all weather conditions as well as specimen collection. Unfortunately he can't control the weather as you see we have a huge storm heading our way."

"Very nice to meet you Doctors. Yes you're right. It does look like a bad one rolling in." David Lynch laughs while expressing his thoughts about the cold weather. "Too bad Dr. Petit you couldn't control the weather, I would put an order in for a sandy warm beach front. You really must do research on a beach someday, then count me in for that trip."

All four men begin to laugh at the light humor David Lynch offers up to break the ice. Dr. Petit is quick witted himself offering his own take of research on a beach.

"I think your right Mr. Lynch, research on a beach would be right up my alley however, I don't think any work would get done with all the beautiful distractions walking around."

After the formalities are done, Dr. Aurora shows the two men to their ride that will take all of them to the main base. Everyone climbs in the Polar vehicles and are now on their way. Meanwhile, Dr. Hendricks is preparing a report finalization for the corporate team arriving that would be a summation for the last quarter statistics. He peers out his window that is frosted, but can still make out images approaching the Station and sees the team arriving back to base. The Polar #1 and #2 vehicles arrive and the men are now walking into the main building that also acts as the scientific laboratory for everyone. Dr. Hendricks leaves his office to greet the visitors along with the other Scientists.

"Welcome gentlemen to Station Zebra! As some might elude to the "Zoo" Dr. Hendricks also tries his hand at being a comedian, but falls short at doing so at times. "I take your travels were of a safe one."

Dr. Petit introduces Mr. Lynch and Mr. Giles to the rest of the scientific team that are there to greet them. "Well gentlemen. This is our esteemed leader Dr. Alan Hendricks. He is the harsh slave task master that keeps the brains of the outfit working like clockwork."

"Oh don't let Dr. Petit make you think anything other than I am a real jolly fellow." Dr. Hendricks smiles as he shakes the hands of both men.

"This is our junior on the team, Dr. Sarah Burns. She is our systems data collector, however, at times I think she is trying to figure all of us out with all this madness going on."

"Someone has to keep all these old scientist on their toes" Laughter breaks out within the small room everyone has gathered.

Dr. Coulter speaks up before he can be introduced by his colleague. "Hello gentlemen. I won't allow Dr. Petit to introduce me for fear he might leave out some of my good qualities." Again laughter breaks out from everyone. "I am Dr. Joseph Coulter. I handle all the lead demographics for analytical data we collect on specimens up here in the big white north."

Mr. Giles looks around the room after all the introductions are made and asks, "I thought there were six of you working at the Station?"

"Yes your right Mr. Giles." Dr. Hendricks explains. "Dr. Ross is our newest addition to our research team and she is a very hard worker. We couldn't drag her from her work at hand but-."

"Oh don't you make me out to be the bad guy, I mean the bad girl now Dr. Hendricks." Dr. Ross walks in the room just at the right time. "What Dr. Hendricks fails to tell you is, he loads me up with all the reports to write keeping me locked away in my office for hours on end. Hi nice to meet you two, I am Dr. Margaret Ross."

Dr. Hendricks acts surprised and shocked at the statement Dr. Ross has just said. "My word! If I didn't hear that with my own ears, I would have thought you were accusing me of being like scrooge at Christmas time."

"Dr., look around you, after all its like Christmas here twenty-four-seven, three hundred and sixty five days out of the year. What would have ever given you that idea" Dr. Ross pauses then breaks out in laughter along with everyone else as the light hearted fun and introductions have now all come to a close.

"Well with all that said and done gentlemen, I am sure you are exhausted from your long trip to our exotic tropical paradise. Alan, Dr. Coulter here, will show you to your rooms. Oh, don't worry about the formalities in titles with us up here, you can call us all by our first name if you wish. We will meet up later this evening after dinner to go over things. Rest well gentlemen, we will talk much later yes?" Dr. Hendricks and the others start to leave the meeting room as Dr. Coulter takes the two men to their rooms to rest from their long travel.

Dr. Hendricks, Dr. Aurora, and Dr. Petit convene to the lounge to discuss the difference in data readings they have been receiving over the last few days. As well, they have noticed a strange phenomenon happening near the Luzon Ice Shelf roughly 10 miles from Zebra Station. Strange sounds and lights have been recorded on several occasions during testing times, which has the scientists concerned. They have managed to capture a single photograph that Dr. Ross is about to show them, as she has finally developed the negatives in the dark room.

Robbie Thomas

Dr. Hendricks asks Dr. Aurora about the final analysis from the testing they did on the sound data from last night. "Jun, did you run the data from last night comparing it to the last four tests?"

"Yes. Here are the spreadsheets on the analysis." Dr. Aurora hands copies of his findings to the other to overlook. "What I find extremely odd is, at several times during the testing there is a low frequency hum that is consistent throughout in length each time it happens. Here, here, here and one more time here."

Dr. Aurora looks on intensely. "I would like to compare the difference in temperatures at the time each interval happened. Leon, what were your readings at those specific times?"

"During the first and let me see, yes, actually during each time the temperature did change in the testing area along the Luzon Ice Shelf. It changed dramatically. The temperature increased by ten degrees during a thirty second burst. Then as soon as it happened, it decreased by ten degrees immediately after."

The three scientists are looking at all the paperwork and data sheets on the table in front of them. Dr. Petit continues to speak about more data he collected of specimen samples of the ice.

"What I found extremely odd is, if you look at my samples here and here, the collected carbon in the ice during extraction it much higher. Now, look at the extraction that was collected after the sound and temperature increase, it's much denser."

Dr. Hendricks pauses in thought looking at the data. "Leon what do you make of this?"

Time Shift – The Paradigm

"Well, I have never in my career experienced anything like this. I really don't know what to make of it. Jun, now looking at your data and the time frame of each, now this is just a guess, but I would say gentlemen we are experiencing a new strange phenomena that no man has ever seen or heard of before." Dr. Petit is now looking at the other two Dr.'s who are very attentive to what he is saying.

Dr. Hendricks puts his hand on his face thinking of all the collected data. As the three of them are going over the information, the door to the lounge flings opens and Dr. Burns comes running in with news of something she has recorded.

"Guys, you're not going to believe this! The other night during taking photos while we were doing all the testing, I was able to record a bit of sound from my recorder while I snapped a few photos. Here listen to this."

Dr. Burns pushes play on the recorder, the ten second burst of sound leaves goose bumps with the other Doctors listening. The eerie sounds have embedded themselves raising eyebrows as to what was it that Dr. Burns has captured.

"Sarah, what was that?"

"I have no idea Alan, but it was captured the exact time of the fluctuations of temps that Leon recorded."

"This all has to be comparable to the specimen collection as well then. Each time those temperatures rose that we gathered, which we see on the data sheets, they also align with what Sarah has. It's all becoming very interesting!" Dr. Aurora explains.

Sarah is anxious to show everyone the photo she captured as well. "Here, you really have to see this! I captured this during the last burst of that sound. I

Robbie Thomas

Time Shift – The Paradigm

decided to grab the camera snapping a few shots in the direction of the sound and well, you tell me what you see!"

The three of them are now looking at what Dr. Burns has captured on her camera. They are totally shocked. The lounge has now become very quiet as the three men just stare at the photograph.

"We have to show this to the others!" Dr. Hendricks quietly explains. "You see what I see. This is remarkable indeed."

Suddenly there is a very strong tremor that lasts only for a few seconds. Just as fast as it started, it comes to an abrupt finish with a thunderous cracking sound that echoes from the Luzon Ice Shelf. The four Doctors are tussled about from the earthquake as there is some damage done to the building they are in. They are now regaining their footing checking out if everyone in the room is ok. The room suffers minor damage as pictures and books from shelves are tossed the floor.

"Is everyone ok? Is anyone hurt at all?" Dr. Hendricks asks.

The other three get up and brush themselves off looking around the room at things thrown about.

"Alan, in all the years we have been up here that has never happened before!" Dr. Petit states. "What do you think caused that?"

"I'll check on the others." Dr. Burns runs out of the lounge.

"I think we should assemble a small team to check out our collection pods near the Luzon Ice Shelf. Hopefully they haven't been disturbed." Said Dr. Petit.

"I'll come with you Leon and we'll take Margaret" Dr. Aurora smiles sarcastically, "It will give the rookie a chance to see the pods for the first time."

Robbie Thomas

"You know Jun, you're going to make my new understudy quit on me. Be gentle on her would you! Ok gentlemen please be careful and-."

Dr. Aurora cuts Dr. Hendricks off in a playful way. "Yes, we know! Check in every half hour to make sure we are all ok. When are you going to learn to relax? You're going to give yourself a heart attack."

Dr. Petit picks up Dr. Hendricks Plaque that has fallen off the wall and hands it to Dr. Aurora while he continues to make light of the situation. "Either that or die from an earthquake!" The three men start to laugh which lightens the mood.

Station Zebra is now active with much going on right after that small devastating earthquake. A team is organizing to head out to the Luzon Ice Shelf to check the research pods that are stationed at various points collecting data. The trek will take them the better part of the day to arrive at their objective. As the team begins to pack up the Polar #1 and Polar #2 vehicles with vital equipment, they take notice to the large storm still approaching. The four team members are now boarding the Polar vehicles and are departing Station Zebra on the slow trek that will take them to the most dangerous part of the North Pole.

The two new comers look on discussing the expedition taking place. Nathan Giles, still shaking from just arriving from a long trip, then experiencing a small earthquake, leaves him stunned. He is having second thoughts of even being brought on this trip by the Chardon Corporation.

"Doctor, you don't think this is a bad omen do you? I mean, with that storm approaching plus we just experienced an earthquake." Nathan continues to watch as the expedition party departs from the base. "I have a bad feeling about this!"

Robbie Thomas

Dr. Hendricks smiles at Nathan Giles thoughts about what is going on. "Mr. Giles, I assure you, there is absolutely nothing wrong or out of the ordinary!" Dr. Hendricks wipes the frost from the window to keep a clear look at the team leaving. "They are the best of the best in the scientific field. That small earthquake is just part of the movement that is natural by mother earth, nothing to worry about."

"See told you Nathan there is nothing to worry about, we are in good hands." David Lynch is trying to convince his partner while looking at Dr. Hendricks. "I am sure if there was something to worry about the good Dr. here would have warned us about it by now, right Dr.?"

"Absolutely Mr. Lynch, there is nothing to worry about at all. Now come with me you two, you must be famished after taking such a long flight. Let's go see what we can rustle up in the kitchen shall we?"

The three men start down the hallway of the main building towards the kitchen area to prepare some dinner for themselves. Dr. Hendricks is trying to take their focus away from the small tremor they have experienced and the outlook of the storm that is approaching.

The team that has now set out towards the Luzon Ice Shelf is in contact with each other over the radio. They discuss instrumentation readings they are currently picking up as they approach the first data pod. Dr. Ross is analyzing data coming into the Polar Two while confirming with Dr. Aurora who is at the wheel.

"Leon, I am getting seismic readings coming into us just now. Are you guys picking this up in Polar One?"

"Yes Sarah, we are also picking up the activity. It's small, must be a small aftershock. We will probably experience many of them for a bit now after having that larger one not long ago."

Dr. Burns alerts the team over the radio of the first Data Pod. "Ok guys, we're here! The first pod is just up ahead about twenty meters. Let's get this one secured and collect the data then head to the second one ASAP. I don't like this storm that is coming in." Dr. Burns turns her headset off for a moment to talk to Dr. Petit. "I don't like being out here with that phenomena thing we captured last time. It gives me the heebie jeebie's!"

"I think it was just a fluke happening Sarah, although, the photo's and recordings were exceptional. Freaky things happen up here at the North Pole, come on you know that!"

"I'm not stupid Leon. You know just as well as I do, there is something happening and I don't want to be around when it does. I'm just saying!"

"You really have to lay off the caffeine Sarah. Decaf remember decaf."

Dr. Burns looks funny at Dr. Petit as he comes to a stop at the first pod. "You're so funny, one million comedians out of work and I happen to be stuck with the only one up at the North Pole. How convenient."

Leon laughs. "Oh you love it and you know it!"

The four team members are now braving the cold, as they open the first pod to collect the data while checking out the area for any damage done by the tremor. The storm is now just upon them closing in fast. The temperature is dropping making working in the cold very difficult for more than 5 minutes at a time. The first pod had no damage sustained from the earthquake while the data was

Robbie Thomas

inconclusive, which makes the scientific team a bit baffled on the information collected.

They all are back in their Polar Vehicles heading to the second data pod, which is a quarter of a mile away from the first, bringing them closer to the Ice Shelf. Temperatures are now very low, as the storm is striking with force making it very difficult to drive in the white outs that are occurring. This is hampering the expedition while slowing the progress of collecting all the information they need in order to determine the disposition of the Luzon Ice Shelf area.

Dr. Aurora wants a reading on the atmospheric pressure. "Maggie, what do you have for a pressure check? Doesn't this storm look a bit off to you?" Dr. Aurora is driving very slow due to the white out conditions and looking at the storm they are all involved in. "Something really doesn't seem right, what do you think?"

"I have never seen anything like this before Jun! This is most certainly a storm of the century. The pressure is reflecting that! Look, this is odd!" Dr. Ross shows the read out to Dr. Aurora who is totally taken back.

"Ok let's get to the second pod collect what we have too and get out of town fast. I have never seen readings like this before. What do you make of it?"

"I have no idea! Your guess is as good as mine." Dr. Ross continues to look at the instrumentation and then radios Polar 1. "Ladies and gentlemen, with the conditions outside as they are we better hurry to finish our work and get back to Zebra Station." Dr. Ross glances one more time at the data they are receiving in Polar Two then asks Dr. Aurora to stop the vehicle. "I think Jun, you better take a look at this! Stop here for a second."

Robbie Thomas

"Stop?! Are you sure? We are almost there!"

"Yes, you have to look at this!"

Dr. Aurora stops the Polar Two as the others in Polar One also do the same.

"Ok Maggie, what do you have there?"

"Look at the readings from before we left, compared to us approaching pod #1 and now as we near data pod #2. Temperatures are all over the map. Atmospheric pressure doing the same, but this is extraordinary. Look at the sound data coming in. There has been a constant hum just up until we arrive closer to the ice shelf." Dr. Ross points to the difference in all the new data she is collecting as both her and Dr. Aurora observe it.

Polar One radios to Polar Two. "Hey, this is no time to stop for a picnic! What's up you guys." Dr. Burns makes light of the situation then laughs with Dr. Petit.

"Leon, have you guys noticed at all the change in the temps, pressure and now this is really strange, but the sound vibration data is changing as well. Jun and I think something is happening what do you think?"

Dr. Burns looks at the data they are getting as well. "She's right! Look at this. Dr. Burns continues to look at the collection of information within Polar 1 with Dr. Petit.

"What do you make of it Maggie?"

"I don't know what to say. This is strange!"

Dr. Burns radios back to Polar Two. "Look lets continue on route to pod #2 keeping an eye on all the data coming in. If it continues, we should radio back to

Zebra all our findings sending it to Dr. Hendricks."

"I agree. Ok we should go get pod #2 info and see what's waiting there for us." Dr. Aurora feels something isn't right. "Let's just hope we make it there without incident."

The two Polar Vehicles start their way once again heading towards data pod #2. Its slow moving through the fierce storm they are enduring. As things would have it, Dr. Hendricks is entertaining the two gentlemen from the Chardon Corporation by making dinner while Dr. Coulter joins them.

"Now that's what I'm talking about! You gentlemen don't mind if I join you this evening." Dr. Coulter walks into the kitchen area where he smells the good cooking of Dr. Hendricks.

"Like clockwork I would say!" Dr. Hendricks laughs. "I have yet to see you pass up anything I cook Joseph."

Dr. Coulter smiles continuing the friendly banter while looking at the two corporate gentlemen. "Well you know me Alan, I can't pass up a good thing. Besides you look good in an apron."

David Lynch speaks up about the corporation doing its own cooking of sorts. "That brings me to the thought Doctors. The Chardon Group has decided to trim the fat so to speak and I hate to be the one to break the bad news."

"Are you saying they are thinking on cutting our funding to our project?" Dr. Coulter looks at Dr. Hendricks who is just as surprised. "Why would they want to cut us out? We are so close with so much more research to do."

Nathan Giles doesn't like to break bad news, but now that it is out in the open over dinner, he helps pass along the bad news.

"I'm afraid so. Shareholders are concerned with certain events happening around the world, as well as up here in the North Pole. I am just as disappointed as you are-."

"I wish I could say I share the same sentiment Mr. Giles and Mr. Lynch, however, I strongly feel you're making a grave mistake. We have given everything we have over the years to the corporation and this is how we get treated." Dr. Coulter stands up, slams his coffee cup on the table and walks out of the dining area.

David Lynch looks at his partner Nathan Giles. "Well, that went over really well."

"As well as to be expected Mr. Lynch. What did you expect? To just fly in to our camp, hand us the bad news and everything would just be roses? I must concur with my colleague. The corporation owes us more than a thank you very much but I am sorry we are closing the doors on your work." Dr. Hendricks also gets up from the table placing his diner plate in the dirty dishes tray. "Now if you will excuse me, I have other pressing matters to attend to. I am sure you two know your way to your rooms. Good night gentlemen."

Dr. Hendricks joins Dr. Coulter in his office to discuss the news they were just handed and what is to be expected next. As Dr. Hendricks walks towards Dr. Coulters office, he over hears transmissions of conversations taking place between Polar #1 and #2 expedition teams that are heading towards data pod number 2. He stands and listens to the information being shared about the changes in and around their area, which are seemingly altering drastically in different intervals. He hears something he doesn't like, and then walks down to Dr. Coulter's office to tell him.

"Ah! There you are my friend. I thought I would catch you here."

"You know Alan, they have no right to shut us down. No right at all. After all those years working for them, this is the gratitude we get, that's horse shit."

"I know Joe, this is not a moment to remember that's for sure. We have given them the better part of our lives doing their research. I know it's maddening."

"It's bullshit! That's what it is! Who the hell do they think they are?!" Dr. Coulter pours Dr. Hendricks a drink from the bottle of scotch he has on his desk. "Now what? What are we going to do now?"

Dr. Hendricks looks at his drink, swirls the glass around as he watches the scotch mix with the ice. "Now? We drink the Scotch and think about it later."

Just as Dr. Hendricks raises his glass to offer a cheer to the accomplishments of the Zebra Station, there is this horrid sound emanating throughout the base. It is a deep moaning sound, which shakes the very souls of the Doctors sitting there. Suddenly a large violent earthquake grabs hold of the Station shaking it like never before. Parts of the buildings on base are collapsing. As suddenly as it all began, it stops. The two Doctors look at each other and immediately head to the radio room. They run down the hallway jumping over debris that has either fallen off the walls or from shelves.

Dr. Coulter jumps on the radio trying to contact the two Polar Vehicles retrieving the information at the pods. It's useless as they can only listen in and can't transmit back to them. The two listen to the horrific sounds along with the frightening moments that are being transmitted back and forth.

Robbie Thomas

"Oh My God!"

"Leon!"

"Sarah! No!"

The voice of Dr. Ross can be heard screaming their names over the radio.

"Help us please! Maggie, you've got to help us..."

Dr. Burns is hurt and trying to call out for help as Dr. Petit is unconscious in Polar 1. The vehicle is and has fallen between a crevasse stuck down thirty feet wedged between the large opening that just occurred.

"Leon... Leon! Oh God please no. No, no, no!"

There is a slight pause as Sarah looks around noticing the entire situation of what has just happened. She warns the others not to attempt to come close.

"Maggie look, you can't come close, it's too dangerous. Leon is hurt bad. He's not responding..." She looks down at her leg, "I think my leg is broken."

Dr. Burns looks down at her leg noticing a steady flow of blood coming from the tear in her thermal protective snow suit. She grabs her leg and lets out an agonizing scream of pain. She sits for a moment collecting her thoughts crying, knowing there's absolutely nothing the other two Doctors are going to be able to do to help them.

"Sarah, you sit tight. We're going to get you out of there." Dr. Aurora talks to her on the radio. "Try not to move around too much ok?"

"What are we going to do Jun? How are we going to get them out of there?" Dr. Ross says frantically.

"I don't know... Let me think."

"Jun, we have to get them out of there. This can't be happening."

"Maggie, we don't have any rope or cables. We have absolutely nothing to help them."

Maggie is not accepting this and can't believe what she's seeing. "This can't be happening right now!" Maggie screams out in anger. "This is not fucking happening!"

Dr. Aurora looks out the vehicles window toward the Luzon Ice Shelf noticing the paranormal phenomena taking place, but can't quite make out what it is and he is stunned at what he sees. He can't speak, but manages to hit Dr. Burns on the arm to get her attention to look at what he is seeing.

"What the hell is that?!"

"I don't know. It's like looking through a veil or mirror. What the hell?!"

Just as the two are looking at the paranormal phenomena closing in on them, there is movement of the displaced crevasse. As both quickly look towards where Polar 1 has fallen with Dr. Petit and Dr. Burns, there is one loud scream from Dr. Burns as the vehicle slips into the dark abyss.

"No Sarah! What the fuck just happened? This is not happening, Jun!" Dr. Ross cries as Dr. Aurora holds her in disbelief. Their colleagues have just lost their lives falling into the unknown.

Dr. Hendricks and Dr. Coulter can't believe what they're hearing. There's absolutely nothing they can do to help, as horrific sounds of their colleagues are heard over the speakers in the radio room. They feel helpless, as there are no other vehicles available to bring help to those out in the storm. There is a deep empty feeling of despair that has come over both Dr.'s. They know there is no way to communicate with anyone at all over the radio. They sit there staring into the radio waiting to hear anyone's voice that might break the silence, which has now consumed them.

Dr. Aurora decides to film what they are seeing. It's approaching them at a rather fast pace. Dr. Ross pulls herself together long enough to assist Dr. Aurora by holding the camera, while he describes what they are encountering.

"Are we on? Make sure you get this behind me Maggie."

"We're rolling. Go ahead."

Dr. Aurora is trying to speak with the cold wind picking up blowing into his face. The whiteout conditions are more frequent now happening all around them.

"If you can see this and hear me, Dr. Margaret Ross is filming while I will try to explain what happened here and what is happening now." The roar of what sounds like a train heading directly towards the two Doctors, is starting to engulf everything around them. "We've had a terrible accident near data pod #2. Dr. Petit and Dr. Burns have fallen into a crevasse which has taken their lives. There was absolutely nothing we could have done to save them."

"Jun, behind you!" Dr. Ross screams for him to take a look at the movement of the phenomena. She can't believe her eyes as she finally is getting a much clearer focus through the whiteout of what it is that is headed for them. "What the hell is that?!"

Dr. Aurora turns to look through the whiteout of blowing show. He is terrified at what he sees as his eyes open wide looking into the hourglass of time and space! "If you can see this Dr. Hendricks, this is remarkable! Maggie! Film it. If you can see what we're seeing, this looks to me like a mirrored doorway of some sort. I can see…yes, I can see through it!" Dr. Aurora pauses for a moment trying to catch his breath from the cold wind blowing and trying to focus more on what it is that is bearing down on them.

Maggie is still filming and can't believe what she is catching on film. She has a hard time speaking because of the force of the wind in her face. "I can see another life. It looks like…it looks like another world-."

"Are you getting this Maggie? What in the world?" Dr. Aurora yells out.

"We have to upload this now Jun! We are running out of time."

"Yes, immediately upload it and send it to Dr. Hendricks!"

The two Doctors enter back into Polar Vehicle #2 to upload the footage they have just filmed sending it to Dr. Hendricks. They are very apprehensive, as whatever it is that is coming directly for them seems to be devouring everything in its path. Dr. Ross is hurrying trying to plug in the USB Cord to the equipment in the vehicle. The download is taking a bit of time, while the time that they don't have is escaping them fast. As this mysterious phenomenon is now very close to them the download is finally complete. They have sent it to Dr. Hendricks back at Zebra Station successfully. Unfortunately, it's too late for them to escape the wrath of the paranormal event about to take place.

"I'm sorry things have to be this way Maggie. There is nothing we can do now to outrun this thing." Dr. Aurora leans against the inside of the cab looking out at what is about to take their lives.

Robbie Thomas

Dr. Ross is silently looking at Dr. Aurora with tears filling her eyes, as she knows this will be the end. "Me too!"

Within less than a minute they are swallowed up by the mysterious phenomenon that has ascended upon them. All that remains is the loud roar from this monster event. The hallowed sounds of nothingness has claimed even more victims, moving ever closer to Zebra Station.

Dr. Hendricks, along with Dr. Coulter, is awaiting the film footage to upload on their computer system in the radio room. Both can't believe everything that has transpired with the loss of their four colleagues. Silence has now befallen the Zebra Station as the download is complete. They will be able to see what has happened and headed their way.

David Lynch along with Nathan Giles, have now entered the radio room standing by the door watching the horror unfolding as the video begins to play on the computer. Everyone sits attentively staring at the screen with no words spoken as numbness has crept into their very souls.

"What are you going to do Doctors? This, whatever it is, is headed right for us!" Nathan Giles in a very scared voice speaks up. "We just can't sit here! What are we going to do?"

Dr. Coulter and Dr. Hendricks look at each other as to concede to what will be their final moments at Station Zebra. Dr. Hendricks takes the video from the file, attaches it to an email addressed to the White House direct mailing for the President of the United States. He hits enter complacently and then turns to his longtime friend and colleague Dr. Coulter.

"Do you have any more of that good Scotch you been hiding behind that fake bookshelf you have in your office?"

"I believe I do! Let's see about having a glass or two, Alan."

As the two Doctors start to walk out of the radio room knowing their fate is sealed with whatever the phenomena is that will soon consume Zebra Station, the two corporate gentlemen are frantic with nothing being done to save them.

"Scotch, at a time like this? Dr., I suggest you do something. What are we going to do?" David Lynch's voice cracks under pressure knowing that their time has come to face uncertainty.

Dr. Coulter stops, walks up to the two men and waits for an answer. "What do you mean, what are WE going to do?! I don't know about you two corporate boys but I think your careers are about to come to an end!" Dr. Coulter just smiles looking at the two standing there with fear in their eyes.

"Well, how about that drink Alan? Shall we?"

"Yes by all means Joe. Do you remember that time we were in New Zealand..."

The two doctors can be heard reminiscing about their adventures as they leave the radio room while the Paranormal Phenomena begins to engulf Zebra Station along with its inhabitants. The darkness of the unknown has come to claim those left at the Zebra Station. The eerie silence is all that remains as the hallowed winds blow throughout the area. Nothing moves, for nothing is anymore!

Robbie Thomas

Digging up Ruins

Professor Elizabeth Ross and her team are organizing their next steps and planning a research party to investigate the area in which this dimensional mirrored image came from. Also they are awaiting arrival of Professor Gates and Wright as they are accompanied by Captain McGuire from the United States Marines. The tension at base camp has everyone on edge, for they don't know what they are up against and what is awaiting them.

During the events that took place through the night, Professor Ross as well as her team was able to record the sounds and happenings that were occurring from the ongoing shift, which is now encompassing the Jungle of Peru. The air of mystery gives way to all the natural sounds the jungle offers each night, however, something has silenced it.

Ross is detailing what provisions are needed for the trip with Miguel, one of the team members in the meeting tent at base camp. They are gathering necessary items they will take along for the hike to the area in which they captured the photograph of a mirrored image. Steven is an assistant to Professor Ross and together they are organizing the expedition and mapping out the areas in which to investigate.

Ross is grabbing a backpack putting essentials in it for the trek to the area. "Miguel...veinen aqui por favor (in Spanish: come here please). Steven, we need to establish a new area for a second base camp closer to the intersection of the axis of this event."

Steven is also collecting things for the expedition and answers Professor

Ross. "It's being taken care of as we speak. You know Beth, I don't think it's such a good idea to be so close to ground zero."

Hurrying to pack her bag, Ross stops and looks at Steven. "Oh come on Steven, where is your sense of adventure. You know as long as I've known you, you've never been so apprehensive about seeking a new find. What's wrong with you?"

Steven stops what he is doing and looks around the campsite. "Beth, I don't know if you were looking at what all of us have seen and are seeing, but this isn't a find, this has found us. I know each of us at base camp love you and your work but this is beyond what we have set out to do. We really should leave this to those coming to figure it out."

Ross puts down her backpack and walks over to Steven putting her hands on his arms. "Steven, come on. Do you remember the time in Mexico when you and I were encountered with what some were calling a UFO experience of the century? What happened to that adventurous guy I know. You're not spooked are you? Just think of it as a new adventure. Besides, do you know what this would mean for our expedition here in Peru? We would be funded through the ears on a new find this essential. Now that news would break around the world with great importance."

Miguel one of the workers under Professor Ross enters her tent. "Si el Professor Ross." (in Spanish: Yes Professor Ross)

Ross smiles at Miguel, and then looks back at Steven. "See Steven, take Miguel here. Not scared of a little ground shaking, or even the crack of thunder and he is so ready to check it out. You know thousands of years their people were

Time Shift – The Paradigm

investigators and conquerors. Don't be afraid of something as little as what we witnessed Steven, it's a new find, just think of it."

Steven is still very apprehensive about the whole ordeal and tries to explain. "Beth, I know what you're getting at but-"

Ross turns to Miguel waiting for her orders walks over towards him while looking at Steven. "Miguel, decirle al senor Avery aqui' lo que su gusto a ser objeto de caza y la caza de un!" (in Spanish: Miguel, tell Mr. Avery what it's like to be hunted and to be the hunter.)

Miguel looks at Steven in a very serious way. He takes a dramatic stance and explains exactly what Professor Ross wanted Steven to hear. "Si el Professor Ross. La ejecucion de caza miedo, el cazador se ejecuta con el hambre en su corazon para conquistar." (in Spanish: The hunted run scared, the hunter runs with hunger in his heart to conquer.)

Steven who is not buying the theatrics sarcastically replies. "Yah, yah I know. The hunted run scared and the hunter runs hungry to conquer. But Beth, we don't know what that is out there, for all we know it could be the death of us."

Time is getting on so Professor Ross ends the fun and starts to get serious. "Miguel, toma esto y lo puso con el resto de los suministros, gracias." (in Spanish: Miguel, take this and put it with the rest of the supplies, thank you.)

Miguel quickly takes what is given him from the Professor. "Ningun profesor problema, su bienvenida." (No problem professor, you're welcome.)

Ross once again addresses Steven's woes. "You see Steven; it's not the fear of being hunted, but the fear of not hunting. Conquer and win Right?"

Robbie Thomas

Time Shift – The Paradigm

As Ross and her assistant are speaking, the sounds of the Helicopters can be heard approaching base camp with Gates and Wright being accompanied with Captain McGuire and his squad. Professor Ross and Steven are now excited to meet the new team members, which will be accompanying them on this new find. The base camp comes alive with everyone milling about getting ready for their arrival.

Steven looks upwards at the sounds of the Helicopters approaching and chuckles at the way Professor Ross wanted to get her point across. "Elizabeth Ross, you sure do have a way with theatrics in explaining things. I could almost say that was an academy award winning moment."

Ross just smiles at Steven as she is anxious to meet the incoming team. I think this is our new team coming in. Let's go meet them. I'm sure they'll want a full briefing on what is going on. Academy award, huh? You might have us doing a new job soon, keep it up Steven, I'll make you a star!"

Steven smiles back saying, "Right! I'll take Jose' and Miguel down to the clearing to get them. Beth, I just want to say...it's always a pleasure uncovering new finds with you, I just...well-"

Ross interrupts the long speech Steven is stumbling into and assures him. "It's fine Steven, I understand. Get out of here and get the new team."

The Helicopter approaches base camp and can be heard from those on the ground. A team has assembled to meet them as they land in the clearing. During the flight to the camp, Captain McGuire along with the Professors discuss their approach and what they expect to find. This is a whole entirely new operation for the Special Operations Commander and his team, so he wants as much information from

Time Shift – The Paradigm

the professors as he can get.

McGuire states to the Professors they are on final approach. "Professor Gates, we are about to land sir. I would appreciate if you and Professor Wright stay close keeping me up to date on what is going on at all times please."

Gates looks at the different weapons the Special Ops are bringing along with them. "Captain, are all these guns really necessary? I mean, we're not going into battle or anything, it's just a new find, an archaeological find."

McGuire with a stern look, stares at the Professor for a brief moment turns to look at his men then back to Professor Gates. "Professor Gates, with all due respect sir, you do your job that you're here for and you leave the military aspect to me. We don't know what we are up against and until we do, I think its best you just stick to research for now."

Sgt. Fisher relays a message to Captain McGuire about the rest of the team. "Sir, Team Objective on the ground is on route sir, confirmation made."

Captain McGuire confirms with Sgt. Fisher. "Roger that. Be sure Taylor and Baker check the perimeter for hostiles."

"Roger that, Sir!"

McGuire reaches into his vest pocket and pulls out two capsules. "Professors, take this and swallow it. It's not a drug and it won't hurt you. It's a highly sophisticated GPS Tracking chip, which will allow us to track you completely around the world. It's a precaution in case something happens."

Wright looks at what has been handed him, then looks at Professor Gates with a real concern look on his face. "Captain, is this really necessary?"

Robbie Thomas

"Professor Wright, we don't know what type of hostiles we are dealing with down there. If you go missing, this will help us find you within minutes. It's either taking this, and if something happens we get to you or if not, well, you're on your own."

The two professors look at one another just after Captain McGuire explains what could happen, and then proceed to swallow the capsule GPS chip given them. The helicopter now lands on the ground in the clearing where the camp team is waiting for them. There is a yellow smoke screen that has been placed to outline the area for the new landing party.

McGuire orders Fisher to help make sure the area is safe. "Fisher, secure the perimeter with the ground team. Set a perimeter of one hundred yards from base camp."

"Roger that!"

Gates and Write now exit the helicopter and are met by Professor Ross's assistant Steven. "Professors Gates and Wright, it's very nice to see you again. You're looking rather well. How was your flight?"

"Steven, it's quite nice to see you again too my friend." Professor Gates replies.

Wright concurs the thought and shakes Stevens hand. " Hello Steven, keeping busy I hear."

"Well you know Elizabeth, always on the go. There's never a dull moment working with her!"

Wright laughs. "Indeed! That woman has more get up and go than all of us put together. Sometimes I wonder where she gets all her energy."

McGuire politely interjects. "Ok Gentlemen. Let's get out from the clearing and take cover over there." He points in another direction. "We don't want to be caught with our pants down!"

The team is on the move to the tree line to meet up with the others waiting for them. The professors and Captain McGuire along with Steven, are jogging toward the ground team who are away from the outgoing helicopters.

Steven looks concerned asking Professor David about the huge operation taking place. "David, what's with all the heavy artillery? Is there something I'm missing here?"

"Washington insists. Seems we are to be babysat while we're here uncovering the phenomena out there."

Sgt. Fisher voice can be heard coming over the radio.

"Perimeter secured sir. One hundred yards cleared. Over."

McGuire addresses the two Professors while acknowledges Sgt. Fisher. "Ok Professor, lets head out to base camp. We want to be there before dusk. Fisher, get Taylor and Baker to follow up behind keeping an eye. Over."

The team enters base camp and is greeted by Professor Ross. Light banter is exchanged with hugs and well wishes.

Wright smiles with his arms opened wide as he walks up to greet Ross. "Ah, there she is. You are most certainly a sight for sore eyes young lady! How have you been keeping? Well I hope."

Gates waits his turn then jumps in to also greet Ross. "I didn't realize they let

Time Shift – The Paradigm

such beauty in jungles Michael. So this is where you have been hiding. Good to see

you Elizabeth."

"Now, when did Washington decide to send me such feeble minded old

men? And what is this; you brought the army with you?"

McGuire introduces himself. "Captain McGuire, United States Marines,

Ma'am. We have our orders to escort and help out in this operation at hand."

Elizabeth is inquisitive to know. "When did Washington become so

interested in archaeological finds Captain? This is out of the norm wouldn't you

think?"

McGuire wears an agreeing smile. "It seems what has happened out here

Professor is actually happening around the world. Washington gets involved when

it's a security issue to the United States."

Michael tries to change the seriousness of the conversation. "Yes, that's our

Elizabeth! Hello darling, such a nice residence you keep. I love what you've done to

the place."

Elizabeth still concerned about the presence of the military replies. "Well

you know me Michael, what Mother Nature dishes out; I take in as my home away

from home."

David agrees with a warm look on his face. "I believe she's becoming our

very own jungle bunny. You sure keep yourself hopping Elizabeth. I don't know

how you do it, being out here at the length of time you do."

Elizabeth starts to gather up a few things again to bring along with the

expedition team. "Well, if you weren't so stuck and stuffed up in that class you teach

Robbie Thomas

back home, you probably could learn some real history out here David. This is

where all the action is. There is nothing like getting your hands dirty once in a while

and not so much with chalk and chalk boards."

Michael laughs. "OUCH! She's got you there David."

David smirks at Michael. "Seems of late I've been told I should be in such

finer places, like a jungle in South America, quite fitting I must say."

Elizabeth laughs. "Well, you came to the right place. See, what we are facing

is something I have never seen before. These are some of the recordings we captured

in the last twenty four hours. I think you're going to be intrigued by the whole

ordeal."

Elizabeth reaches for her recorder and turns it on. All in the assembly tent

listen attentively to what is finally starting to play. As the recorder is playing,

Elizabeth again reaches for film footage taken the night before and what was

captured during the strange phenomena.

Elizabeth looks over at McGuire asking him to come closer. "Captain, I think

you might want to see this as well. Come on over and have a look." Elizabeth again

now turns on the captured video footage on the laptop on the table. "Now, this

mirrored image, or the looking glass as Steven likes to call it, shows some defined

areas and locations that are distorted. However, if we use the spectra lens ... Well,

you tell me!"

Michael looks intensely at what is being shown. "It most certainly looks like

something, but Washington, Elizabeth I don't know...are you sure?"

David speaks up. "From the photograph you sent to Michael it was very distorted and blurred, but it did resemble Washington."

Elizabeth holding back on her feelings and what she wants to really say, lets everyone adjust to what is being shown to them. "Right! Then we took this with the spectra lens adding infrared, now what do you see?"

Elizabeth then shows them the recording from the high tech Spectra Lens Infrared Camera. They are all taken back from what they see. They all go silent and look at one another.

David can't believe what is being shown. "Oh my God!"

Michael takes his glasses off and slowly leans closer to the laptop. "This is incredible. Remarkable to say the least, do you have any other data as of yet?"

Captain McGuire squints his eyes and can't believe what he's seeing. "Are you saying that thing out there, whatever you call it, is showing us our capital destroyed?"

Elizabeth stands up looking at everyone in the tent and the expressions on their faces. "The only other mentionable data would be what we have been sharing with NASA, other than that, that's all we all know for now. I don't know if that is exactly what I would call Washington destroyed Captain McGuire, but I am sure if we analyze whatever this phenomena is, we will learn from it."

David turns to look at Elizabeth. "Alright then. What are the plans Elizabeth, and when do we go to the event site?"

Elizabeth starts to reach for her things she is getting ready for the hike towards the Phenomena. "José and Miguel have been packing up a few things for the trek, but before we go I want you two to see something. Follow me."

Time Shift – The Paradigm

     Elizabeth takes Michael and David along with Captain McGuire to a new find of her's that has her very puzzled. In fact it is piece of a puzzle from a tablet that contains Hieroglyphics that are a warning of some sort. David being a Historian and Scientist, he has a huge background in ancient writings and is very excited in seeing what Elizabeth has in store for them. They all leave the meeting tent and take a small walk to the back of base camp where Elizabeth has a new find that she is about to show them. This is something the world has been waiting for. For centuries, mankind has been uncovering many ancient artifacts that have many hidden meanings or messages. Now the world will come to know what secrets Professor Elizabeth Ross has uncovered and what they hold for mankind.

Robbie Thomas

The Find

Elizabeth leads the team through the dense jungle to a clearing where they have uncovered a strange new find. As the excitement builds from all who now want to see what Elizabeth has to show them, the air itself is filled with anxiety and the ominous feeling, suspense and intrigue. As they walk the small trail that is laden with broken branches from the brush, they finally come to the opening of the new clearing where Elizabeth and her crew have discovered the new find.

Michael is pushing branches out of his way as he marches through the small trail following the others. "You're always full of surprises Elizabeth. I don't know how you do it, living out here all the time like you do!"

Elizabeth looks back smiling. "Keeps me young professor... keeps me young. Besides I think it builds character in a person with all this jungle around them. What do you think?"

Michael gets annoyed as branches are slapping him in the face while walking the small trail. "I don't know about that, you can keep it, not for me."

Elizabeth laughs. "It's just up ahead here. You know when the Mayan created these vast cities, the intricacies of everything they did revolved around the science of the stars. It not only allowed them to be precise in measuring out the seasons of the calendar, but it also allowed them the immeasurable talent in aligning each city to a degree within its own longitude and latitude. Just Remarkable people."

Michael looks back at David. "Hmm, I think Harvard might be up for a new History professor soon, what do you say David?"

"Oh rest assured Michael, you won't see me in a stuffy classroom anytime soon, there's much more to discover out here. Besides, I don't think David could handle the competition, it might just hurt his ego!" Elizabeth laughs and so does the rest of the team.

"What? I like my classroom, there's nothing wrong with my classroom, Michael tell her." He mumbles to himself as they all start to walk through the jungle again. "There's nothing wrong with teaching History. I have a great group of kids, a nice stuffy classroom, and all the chalk I want. What's wrong with that?"

They reach a cave site area, where Elizabeth has found the tablet with hieroglyphics written on it. The site is of decay filled with the vines of the Jungle embracing every crevasse and crease of the stones lay in place from many centuries ago. There are different areas unexcavated from the new find that show remarkable markings of sacrifice or ceremonies that took place. Stone markers line the way on each side of this temple area that is still below ground surface. The underlying brush gives way to hidden rocks and markers for the beginning of this temple.

As they get closer, some of the symbols and markings seen on the face of the walls are coming into sight. The architecture and structure that is emerging clearly shows the dated timeline of the Mayans and catch the eye of Professor David Gates. The excitement is now building as they get closer to the dig.

Elizabeth excited to show the new team grins and walks a bit faster now that it is in the clearing ahead. "It's just over here! I've tried to translate what is being said but I'm not quite up on my ancient writings before the dynasty of Mayan." She brushes the hair from her face. "I am hoping David that you can enlighten us on what is written and depicted on some of the wall markings."

Robbie Thomas

Time Shift – The Paradigm

David looks straight ahead becoming anxious to read what is written on the walls. "Before the Mayan you say? That would mean the dynasty before them would have, well would have been-"

Elizabeth interrupts David in mid-sentence excitedly. "Not would have been, but rather would be the actual Mayan existence of where it all began! I feel it predetermines everything we come to know about this culture. Well, here you go! Professors, I'd like to introduce to you the words from the civilization as we know them, the Mayan."

Elizabeth uncovers a huge tablet that is lodged in the side of a wall that leaves Michael and David looking on in awe. The mystic of the writing has both professors staring really hard in trying to figure out what it says. The hieroglyphics are of different origin mixed, with the commonly known era of the Mayan to which it has really captured the attention of the two professors. These are new and delicately inscribed stories that have never been seen before. David and Michael both gaze upon the new find Elizabeth has uncovered before them leaving them breathless.

The markings detail many different subsequent events that predate the Mayan Calendar, giving way that possibly the civilization before this great dynasty was not of this world. Many aspects David is now looking at are hard to read and a new language he is having a hard time understanding along with interpreting for everyone standing there.

David is very excited about what he is seeing. "Elizabeth, this is remarkable, simply outstanding… Look at this! The writing itself is a bit difficult, but still

Robbie Thomas

resembles much of what the Mayan literature would have been in the early Mayan Dynasty."

Michael's also very amazed at what he's seeing. He points to a few hieroglyphs. "Exquisite indeed! This, which we are looking at my friends, is truly a great piece of history. Just look at the outstanding markings."

David quickly adds to what Michael is saying as he rubs his hands on the tablet to remove some of the sand that is laying on it. "This writing is a bit different, but nevertheless, it seems to be just pre-Mayan or possibly one of the earliest writings from the Mayan Dynasty." He walks a bit to his left, "Now these ones over here, I have no idea what era they are from. They look to be of some different language altogether!" David slowly turns and looks at Elizabeth and everyone standing there. "Totally a great find Elizabeth, a great find indeed!"

Elizabeth and Michael walk a bit closer looking at what David is pointing out to them. McGuire is amazed at the total surroundings and just looks on. The atmosphere is now reeling with high anticipation if David can make out what is written on the tablet and the walls. David once again brushes his hand over the stone to push away any dirt that lay on the tablet. He tries again to read the language that is before him.

David puts his glasses on and takes a good look. "Yes, well it's a bit different from the known writings of the Mayan but still translatable. Let me see. Hmm, this here, the first five glyphs, they say: 'The time will come, like the night changes day.' No, no wait, that isn't it. Ok here, 'The time will come, when night becomes day and day becomes night.' That's it!"

Robbie Thomas

Elizabeth looks on with anticipation. "Interesting. Keep going."

David points out a few things. "Ok now, this bit here, the next 5 glyphs are a bit harder but lets see; 'when the night consumes all everything is no more. When the night consumes all everything is no more.' Very interesting!"

Michael scratches his head looking at David. "The time will come when night becomes day and day becomes night. When the night consumes all everything is no more,

that's eerie David I assure you. It sounds like a warning of some sort!"

David removes his glasses and looks at everyone standing there waiting for his response. "The Mayan were great story tellers who took great pride in their stone writings. They were the masters of this type which explains how different this tablet is from the earliest I have ever seen or anyone has ever seen for that matter up until now."

Elizabeth is now really interested in getting the rest of the tablet translated. "There is more, can you translate that too?"

David looks at Elizabeth and puts his glasses back on. "But of course, lets see. This over here, is explaining of a way to stop, or prevent would be a better word, a horrible happening from occurring. Let me see. 'Man, beast and the heavens shall be spared when all learn as one.' There seems to be a piece missing. Do you have the remainder of the tablet?"

"No, sorry I don't. This is all we unearthed. It seems to be more of a warning David, than a story." Elizabeth explains.

Michael clears his throat then gives his thoughts. "Yes, it does seem as if it is implying some type of event that took place or is about to take place perhaps."

David agrees with Michael "Good observation Michael. Took place, or about to take place. This is a warning most certainly, however, without the rest of the writing I am unable to determine what it is they are telling or warning us about."

Elizabeth very inquisitive in wanting to know more starts to think. "You're not suggesting this is a warning of the end, or could it be part of what is going on out there now?"

David turns and paces slowly, thinking for a bit. He looks at the writings once more, and then tells everyone what he thinks. "Not suggesting and not disregarding it either. Just look at all the earthquakes, different weather patterns, volcanic activity the polar shift! How about all those sink holes around the world that just magically appeared? Is it a coincidence or are we living their history?"

Michael puts his hand to his face his arm crossed on his chest stares at David and his ability to suggest what he is reading is a prelude to what is going on in the Jungle now. "Surely David, what is happening in most areas of the world can't possibly be connected to what is going on at present. Are you suggesting what we are witnessing in this jungle is what is written on those stones?"

David walks over to Michael putting his hand on his shoulder looking him directly in the eye. "Being a Physicist, I know you're aware of the probable versus the residual. Wouldn't you say, it's a highly educated guess what every historian has said before, that the events have been transcribed by our ancestors. Have they not been nearly one hundred percent accurate, which we relive history over and over since the earliest recordings found by man?"

Robbie Thomas

Just as the professors are engaging in conversation, another large earthquake takes place with once again a loud crack of thunder. The intensity of this earthquake is much more violent as it aggressively moves the earth on the jungle floor with ease. This takes everyone off guard surprising them all. The three professors run for cover entering into the cave like entrance to the temple. The ground shakes so violently that much destruction of the excavation is starting to crumble before them. Captain McGuire along with Sgt. Fisher rushes into the entrance of the temple encouraging everyone to exit as fast as they can before it comes crashing down all around them.

Michael yells out for everyone to take cover. "Hurry, in here! Watch out for the falling rocks."

David pushes on Elizabeth to follow Michael. "Go, go, go!"

Elizabeth screams. "Watch out, David!" but her warning is too little, too late. A   large rock strikes him in the back area knocking him to the ground. As Elizabeth struggles to help him, Michael turns back noticing what has happened to David. Captain McGuire yells out for the three to get out of the excavation area as it is caving in all around them. The walls seem to be just crumbling before their eyes. The ground is shaking violently while taking its revenge on those who are trying to seek shelter from the falling debris. The jungle seems to be moving like a carpet floating on water. The trees are swaying in every direction imaginable. The eerie sound of like metal upon metal crunching together, grinding making a sickening of sounds can be heard coming from deep within the jungle. The earth has come alive seeking victims as it's literally swallowing up everything in its sight.

Robbie Thomas

Time Shift – The Paradigm

McGuire gains his footing reaching for Professor Gates. "Here, grab a hold of my hand. Fisher helps them out over there."

Fisher jumps down from where he was standing to help Elizabeth and Michael. "Come on you two, let's get out of here."

McGuire looks over at the others. "You two ok? Are you hurt?"

They pull together managing to push aside the rocks that have now blocked them from the entrance. They work their way out of the small cave entrance of the temple to the open area outside. Just as they do, there is a small aftershock that completely shakes the remainder of the rocks that were in place, which fall closing the entire entrance of the small opening. The five are thrown once more to the ground in disbelief of what is happening to them. Dust billows up from the rocks falling all around them consuming their very presence leaving a very dense like fog. You can't see your hands in front of your face, as the sounds of rumblings have now succumbed to the echoes throughout the jungle.

Everyone has been tossed around like rag dolls from the massive quake as it ends. A loud crack of thunder breaks throughout the region once more. The five are now starting to tend to each other while assisting Professor Gates as he lay hurt on the ground with cuts to his forehead. Shaken from what just happened to them, they all gather their bearings looking around at the amount of destruction at the excavation site.

Captain McGuire gets to his feet. "Fisher, you ok?"

"Yes sir. I'm fine."

"Ok get back to camp. Check the others. Make sure Baker and Taylor are

Time Shift – The Paradigm

ok. Then get back here on the double."

Fisher picks up his weapon from the ground. "You got it Captain, on my way."

Ross is tending to Gates as he lay on the ground hurt. "David, hold still. Don't move; let me see your head. You seem to have a nasty gash. Captain, do you have anything in your pack."

McGuire reaches into his pack. "Here use whatever you can out of this. It's a first aid kit."

"It's just a scratch. Here, help me up." David tries to get to his feet but has to sit back down in pain. "Oh man that didn't feel right. Ok give me a second, I'll be ok."

Michael walks over to David and kneels down. "I think you better just sit tight buddy. Let Elizabeth check you out and get you fixed up."

David looks up at Michael smiling in pain. "Oh you're not kidding, I feel like I took a fucking beating. Did anyone get the license plate of that truck? Oh man my back. What happened?"

Elizabeth is applying gauze along with bandages to David's neck and head area. "Hold still you old professor while I get this on you. That was one little earth tremor that is for sure. I think you're going to be fine, just let me get this dressing on you."

"Lady, if that was an earth tremor I hate to see what an earthquake looks like. I sure don't want to be around if anything bigger happens or goes off, if you know what I mean." Captain McGuire makes light of the situation.

Robbie Thomas

Michael kind of laughs answering McGuire. "Oh don't take offence Captain. Elizabeth here, she means well, but at times her humor is something to be desired."

Suddenly Fisher radios McGuire in a panic mode. Everyone is listening as they hear the frantic call. Much more has happened back at base camp and now time is of the essence as their attention has to be focused on getting back to camp.

"Captain, this is Fisher. You better get back to camp sir. You have to see this, over."

"What's going on Fisher?"

Fisher slowly looks around at base camp and at the amount of destruction. "Sir, the camp! It's not here!"

McGuire looks at everyone sitting looking back at him as they just heard SGT. Fisher in a frantic voice. "What do you mean Fisher?"

"Sir. It's gone!"

"Ok guys get up and move. Ok Fisher, on our way, secure the area!"

The earth moved swallowing up much in the jungle as it left no mercy in its wake. The silence of the aftermath is deafening as everyone feels something is terribly wrong back at base camp. Their worst nightmares are now coming to life creeping down their necks. Time seems to have come back to take what is properly its owning. They race through the jungle to find out that chaos has ensued while death is upon them. The phenomenon is leaving its calling card while watching from a distance. Time is slowly slipping away leaving the balance of man hanging, as the unknown is making its acquaintance worldwide.

Robbie Thomas

Back to Owensville Kansas

As many things are happening around the world in a major way, Owensville Kansas seems to be the focal point to a bit of a standoff between the phenomena and life as we know it. Many strange occurrences have taken place, but for the most part the town's folk have been kept at bay from becoming part of an ominous outcome. While destruction and mayhem are taking over the planet something of faith is keeping the paranormal mystery from engulfing this town. The military have been running many tests while battling an enemy they have no idea what it is. The White House along with other nations around the world are paying very close attention to Owensville Kansas, hoping whatever it is that is going on there will give some type of resolve for mankind.

Many people from around the world have been lost as cities, villages and more have been consumed leaving no reprieve whatsoever. A special team of experts have been assembled to figure out what if anything can be done to stop anymore of the dark befalling death from taking any more of our existence as we know it. The United Nations have had many emergency meeting in New York, yet no one from any nation has any rational response to dealing with what is going on.

As things are developing elsewhere in the world, Owensville Kansas is holding onto the mere existence as the phenomena watches from a distance. The Sheriff has been racking his thoughts with his Deputy trying not only to keep everything in focus for the town, but that of noticing subtle changes in the people who live there.

"Travis, I am at a loss for trying to figure anything out anymore. What the

hell is that thing out there? Come on get it over with then, come on damn it!"
Higgins yells at the ominous darkness while being exhausted from all that is going
on.

Parker sitting on the ground takes his hat off and rubs his neck. "Yelling at it
ain't gonna get it to go away you know. You're just wasting your time there Dale."

"I know there's nothing any of us can do, but just sit here with it out there
looking at us like it's ready to pounce, I'm sick of it . It's like it wants us to just lie
down and give up" Sheriff Higgins throws a rock in the direction of the mysterious
phenomena. "Fuck you!"

"Well, best we be heading back to town boss. I don't know about you but
I'm done for the day. You know Molly is gonna start to worry about your sorry ass,
so we should call it a night."

"Yah, your right. You know Travis, this is the first time in my life I have felt
utterly useless as a Sheriff. This really sucks big time man."

Parker gets up from sitting on the ground dusts himself off, places his hat
back on his head. "Not much you can do Dale. Hell, the army is just sitting there up
on the ridge and they're not doing much to make things better. Let's just go home
for the night and see what tomorrow brings." Parker gets in the passenger side of the
Sheriffs car.

Sheriff Higgins continues to stare at the mysterious darkness trying to figure
it all out. "Your right Travis. We'll call it a night, I'm not one to argue that point."

Dale gets in his car and begins to drive off leaving the ridge area heading
back to town. He drops his Deputy off at his house wishing him a good night, then

drives off to his own house to be with Molly and his children. As he is driving, he can't help noticing a subtle but weird serene sense emanating from the activity of the mirrored phenomena. Sheriff Higgins arrives at home as Molly is sitting on the front porch with Payton in her lap fast asleep. Dale doesn't notice Molly sitting there in the dark being quiet. He slowly walks up on the front decking to his home trying to be quiet.

"Hey sailor, got a minute?"

"Gosh Molly, you've given me a fright. I didn't see you sitting there."

"Shh…you'll wake Payton. How was your day babe?"

"You know Molly, I have about had it with this thing out there. There isn't anything I can do to get anyone help or get out of this damn town." Sheriff Higgins sits down on the swing next to Molly putting his arm around her. "I am so frigging tired."

"It's not your job Dale. There is a reason the army is right there on the outside of town. Father Murphy said today in mass that we all have to keep the faith-."

"Father Murphy can keep his faith. I like to see his faith take this thing away, but it doesn't look like it's about to happen." Dale stands up to look out into his front yard. That Father Murphy I am so tired of hearing about that man."

Molly knows how much trouble is in Dale's heart and tries to smooth things over. "Why do you always have to be so stubborn? Dale why don't you come to church with us and pray? It gives us peace just knowing."

"Molly, me in church?! That will be the day. No, you just tell that Father

Murphy thanks but no thanks. I'm not about to get stuck in church listening to a bunch of repent or you won't be saved crap! Just look Molly. Look at that thing out there. Do you really think going to church is going to make this go away and everything will go back to normal?"

Molly smiles as she looks at her husband. "God will never turn his back on us Dale, regardless of how bad things get. There is always a lesson to be learned from things like this. You just can't give up."

"Well then Molly! You tell that Father Murphy and God, that I want my town back and life the way it was. If they can do that making this nightmare go away, I will believe. Until then, I need a beer!" Sheriff Higgins walks into his house straight for the refrigerator opening the door. He looks in, grabs a beer flicking off the beer cap with an opener and taking a long drink.

Jessica is sitting in the living room drawing on her sketch pad as Dale walks in and kisses her on the head.

"Hey honey! How was your day?"

"Hi dad! It was good thank you. Didn't do much but glad of what we did though."

Dale grabs a chair in the living room carrying on a conversation with his daughter Jessica. "Oh and what was that Jess?"

"We planted some real nice flowers asking God to give new life to them and as long as they are alive we will be too." Jessica continues to sketch her picture.

"Not you too, Jessie that Father Murphy has you and your mom all convinced that God is going to save us. He has no right-."

"I wouldn't talk like that dad. You know God listens to everything your saying!"

"Well he better hear me now. God are you listening? I need another beer." Sheriff Higgins puts his hand to his ear as to make fun to see if God is talking back. "See Jess, Nothing. Looks like I need to get my own beer."

"Dad, you're funny. But you really shouldn't make fun of God you know."

Dale gets up from his chair and walks to the kitchen for another beer from the refrigerator. "Yah, yah, yah! Ok kiddo, it's almost bed time, be sure to wrap it up and get off to bed now." Sheriff Higgins leans on the counter of the kitchen sink while Molly comes in carrying Payton.

"I'll put him to bed and join you for one. Just give me a minute." She smiles and walks upstairs to put Payton to bed.

Dale takes another swig of his beer while he looks out the kitchen window at all the lights from the military to the north of town. He just isn't sure about things no more, feeling very uneasy at the fact nothing is being done for days now. Molly comes back down from putting Payton to bed, opens the refrigerator grabbing a beer for herself. She hands it to Dale to open for her.

"You really should take time off and stay home with us."

"If I did that, who would keep law and order around here then?"

Molly giggles. "Come on. There is absolutely nothing going to happen. Everyone knows everyone in this town besides, even Travis's wife would like to see him stay home a bit too."

"Oh great. Now it's a freaking conspiracy with you two is it?" Dale walks over to the kitchen table and sits down.

"No honey! Look. The town is pretty much isolated as it is, nothing coming in and nothing going out. What can possibly go wrong?

The Sheriff looks at his wife reluctantly agrees to take a day off to stay home with the family. "Ok, ok! I will take tomorrow off. But that is it! Just tomorrow."

Molly walks over sits on the Sheriffs lap. "Now that is my big brave Sheriff. Now you can help us finish the garden."

Just as Molly starts talking about the garden, Jessica walks into the kitchen. "eww! Gross, cut it out you two! Children live here remember!" Jessica grabs a soda out of the refrigerator and looks at her parents with a funny look as she walks back into the living room. "Really, give it a rest please."

"Your mother and I are going to kiss lots now!" The Sheriff yells out at Jessica as both him and Molly start to laugh.

"Oh Please, give me a break. I am so going to gag!" Jessica yells back at the two in the kitchen.

Molly kisses Dale and gets up walks over to the counter to start to make some dinner for him. She doesn't want to pry into his business but wants to know what is going on with the situation the town is facing.

"Anything new going on with the military on the ridge at all? Have you and Travis been able to figure out what that thing is that is keeping us here?"

"You know there is absolutely nothing I can do. I have no idea what that is or what to do about it. I feel the town has gone morbid and people are doing whatever they want regardless of what I or Travis try to do. It's useless!"

Time Shift – The Paradigm

"People are scared Dale. Everybody is just trying to live their lives with that thing out there. You can't be down on them babe. We are all in the same boat-."

Payton comes walking into the kitchen from waking up from his sleep. "Daddy! I had a dream."

"Hey Payton buddy! Come here boy." Dale reaches out and lifts his son on his lap. "What are you doing awake? Can't sleep?"

"The man came to me and woke me up"

He looks at Molly while talking to Payton. "What man sweetheart?"

"I don't know daddy, it's just a man." Payton yawns and rubs his eyes. "Mommy, can I watch some more T.V.?"

"Yes. Sure you can Payton. Run in the living room and have Jessie put T.V. on for you." Molly goes over taking Payton from the Sheriff and lets him run into the living room.

Dale looks at Molly as he keeps his voice down so the kids don't hear him. "See Molly, this Father Murphy is brainwashing him." He gets up from his chair walks over to the entrance to the living room looks at the kids to make sure they didn't hear him. "Now I got my son telling me he was awakened by a man in his room. This shit has to stop Molly."

Molly, with a slight laugh to her voice says, "Come on Dale! He is just a little boy. He has a big imagination. Besides there isn't anything wrong in believing in Angels from Heaven." Molly grabs the potatoes and begins to peel them.

"Angles from Heaven! A man from Heaven! Molly come on. Give me a break!"

Robbie Thomas

"Dale sometimes you amaze me. Why don't you have some faith for once. Lord knows you could use it! Your son is an innocent little boy who believes. I will be damned, if I let you take that away from him."

"Come on Molly I've had it, I really have. Let's not talk about this shit no more."

"Ok Dale have it your way. Go wash up, I'll have your dinner ready for you in a minute."

"Fine, I am out of here."

The Sheriff takes a last swig of his beer and walks off to wash up before dinner. He starts to make himself a shower when all of the sudden there is a loud crack of thunder and the house begins to shake. Windows are breaking in the home as the alarm goes off. The kids are now crying running into the kitchen where Molly is. She manages to get the kids under the kitchen table to protect them in case of falling objects. The Sheriff tries to get downstairs to his family but falls down the stairs in doing so.

The earthquake stops and there is a bit of damage throughout the home. The kids are frightened as Molly calls out to Dale, but little does she know he is unconscious at the bottom of the stairs in the living room. Molly gains her footing checking the children to make sure they are ok telling them to stay in the kitchen not to move. She calls out to the Dale again as he slowly regains consciousness looking around. Molly finds him at the bottom of the stairs with his back on the floor and his legs up on the stairs dazed from the fall.

"Dale. Are you ok?"

Time Shift – The Paradigm

"Yah I think so. Oh man my back. What the hell was that?" He slowly gets to his feet. "No I'm fine. Are you hurt Molly?"

"I'm alright, the kids are fine too. What is going on Dale?"

"I don't know. I have no idea what that loud thunder was, but that was one hell of an earthquake." They walk back into the kitchen where the kids are.

Molly walks over to the kids hugging them and kissing them. "It's ok. It's all over. Here, sit here. Let me look at you."

Dale walks over the mess in the kitchen looking out his window at the activity of the paranormal phenomena happening in the distance. He can't quite make out what it is, but stares at it while it is changing. The dark ominous mirrored phenomenon is now moving closer to the town growing in size with something a bit different to it. It looks like a mirror you can actually see through to the other side.

"Would you look at that! What the hell?" Dale speaks up. "I have to get a hold of Travis. Look at this thing."

Payton looks at Molly and points to the mysterious mirrored phenomena. "The man from Heaven said its coming mommy. He said it will get us."

Dale hears what his son has just said. He turns to Molly with an expression of having no more patience on his face as to say enough is enough.

Payton looks at his dad and in a soft little boys voice says to him, "Daddy, the man said you need to listen more. He said you need to pray."

"That's it Molly! They do not go to that church no more you hear me." Dale walks out of the house onto his front deck looking at the phenomena to the south that is now growing. He is irate at everything that is going on.

Robbie Thomas

"What the hell are you? What the fuck do you want with us?!" He picks up a rock from the ground throwing it in the direction of the dark phenomena. "Son of a bitch." He falls to the ground from being weak from the fall from the stairs. "Damn it."

As Dale is on the ground still a bit dizzy from being hurt, he looks at his driveway as Travis his Deputy is pulling up.

The Deputy runs over to the Sheriff. "Dale!"

"I am fine, never mind me. How is your family?

"We're fine. A bit shaken but were good. What's going on Dale?"

"Your guess is as good as mine buddy. That thing out there, it's causing all of this shit. Notice it got bigger? Look at it. Just look at it. See anything different?"

Travis stands up looks at it a bit closer. "It looks like you can see through it or something. What do you make of that?"

Dale gets up off the ground looks at the Deputy. "I have no frigging idea. I bet we can get some answers from the military on the ridge. Let's go pay them a visit."

The Sheriff along with the Deputy both jump into the squad car taking off in the direction of the military on the ridge. As they are approaching the ridge they are met by a road block that has been set up more within the perimeter of the town.

"What the-." Travis starts to slow down as he is driving towards the roadblock up ahead.

"Travis I have no idea. I don't like what's going on. This is totally insane man!"

Time Shift – The Paradigm

The ground begins to shake violently once more, as bright lightning along with loud thunder throughout the air itself has changed the landscape. The car is tossed back and forth until the Deputy is able to regain control, bringing it to a stop in the middle of the road. The military just up the road has now come under attack by forces unknown to man. There is a mist thickening throughout the military buildup consuming them, as screams of horror and gunfire can be heard from the roadblock. The dark abyss of mysterious phenomena has now just moved in closer wrapping itself completely around the town, creating a secluded walled area that has everyone trapped. The frightening scene the Sheriff and his Deputy are witnessing has them frozen in their tracks. The two are straight focused as in front of them they witness a supernatural phenomenon unleashing its wrath on everything in its path. Loud sounds of helicopters crashing to the ground as tangled metal shrieks throughout the air followed by hallowed voices calling out in the night for help. A humming sound echoes throughout the valley area leading up to the ridge, this is something no one has ever encountered before. The Sheriff, along with the Deputy are frozen still with their eyes fixated on the strange happening as an ice cold shrill runs through their veins. Heavy breathing comes from both men in the squad car as silence overtakes the moment.

"What the hell just happened?" Deputy Parker in a very low voice asks the Sheriff. "Dale what the fuck is going on here?"

Dale looks around slowly as he swallows his spit in his mouth trying to keep his composure. "Travis, don't move. Don't say anything." The Sheriff doesn't want to draw attention from the strange phenomena to them sitting in the car.

Robbie Thomas

"What are we going to do Sheriff?"

"Slowly get out of the car. Don't shut the door and walk backwards to the tree line."

Dale slowly opens his door putting his right leg out ever so slowly as he slides off the seat to stand up outside the car. The Deputy does the same thing as both men are now standing on the outside of the squad car slowly making their way backwards towards the tree line. The horrific sight of what is taking place is continuing. More screams from military men can be heard like a faint silencing ending abruptly only to claim the next, then the next. The mist continues to thicken while lightning bounces off the inner walls it has created leaving impressions for a brief moment in the dark eerie night sky.

Parker slides down into the small tree line keeping his eyes ever so trained on what is going on in front of him. "Dale, what are we going to do now? It's all around us, its everywhere!"

"Travis, I have no idea. We're going to stay here until there's a break. When that happens then we'll move."

"Sheriff, we have to get back to the town to warn the others." Parker goes to get up, but is suddenly pulled back down by the Sheriff.

"Travis, you go out there now, whatever that is, and you're going to draw it to us." The Sheriff looks around for a way out of the jam they are in. "Let's go through the brush here back to road around the bend back that way. It will give us just that much more of a chance to get away."

The Sheriff and Deputy slowly move back through the brush to the bend in the road far enough away from the event taking place. As they make their way, they are reminded by the horrific silencing of the military as echoing sounds of screams are slowly starting to distance themselves in longer intervals. They make it to the bend in the road and are now walking back towards town. They are in total disbelief of what is happening.

"Travis, do you believe in second chances?"

"I believe everyone deserves some type of chance. It all depends as well as what you consider second chance."

There is a pause as both men continue to walk down the road. They glance back at the mysterious phenomena taking place as the lightening show continues with loud cracks of thunder and the ominous feeling running through their veins.

The Sheriff takes off his hat stops in the middle of the road looking at the Deputy to explain. "Let's say a man sits all his life wondering if he made the right choice. A choice that took only a split second, that changed everything and now wonders if he has a second chance. That man is being eaten up inside just wondering."

Parker looks at the Sheriff pauses with a puzzled look on his face. "If this has anything to do with that kid years ago, you had no choice. There was no second chance in that situation whatsoever. It was either him or you. You gave yourself that second chance back then as far as I'm concerned. You did the right thing."

"He was just a kid Travis. It wasn't supposed to turn out like that."

"I'm not going to sit here letting you beat yourself up about this. That kid did the wrong thing pulling that gun out, it's not your fault. Like I said, it was either him or you and you did the right thing. End of story."

The Sheriff puts his hat back on his head grins at his Deputy as the two continue to walk down the road towards town. The walk takes them roughly an hour to make it back to the center square and they notice a crowd has gathered at the grocery store. They make their way through the crowd into the store where the Mayor is speaking to some of the town's folk.

"Listen, everyone please. Stay calm. I am sure the Sheriff will be here soon. Until then all of you have to remain calm." The Mayor is trying to keep some of the town's folk at ease as they are all frantic of the newly developed events taking place. "Now Sal, you're going to have to wait just like the rest of us. I am quite sure the Sheriff has a logical answer to all of this."

"Logical answer Charlie. Is that what you call it? Who you kidding? That halfwit Sheriff and his side kick can't even write up a proper traffic ticket let alone know what is going on out there. Now we all want answers of what is going on. You're the Mayor of our town or do I have to point out who elected you to that position."

Sal Dickens is working the people into a frenzy who have gathered at the grocery store, which is not impressing the Mayor at all. The crowd is getting a bit upset and restless at the fact nothing is being done to figure out what it is that keeps them prisoner in their own town.

"Please everyone, one at a time." The Mayor is trying to keep them calm, while he notices the Sheriff walking in the store. He waves to the Sheriff to come to the back of the store, where everyone has gathered to speak to the crowd.

"Not a moment too soon. Sal Dickens has worked them all up into a frenzy Dale. Do something about it, I've tried."

"Seems you have handled it pretty good there Mayor." The Sheriff smiles and turns to the crowd that is getting a bit out of hand in the store. "Folks, quiet for a moment. Sal, if you don't behave yourself I will have you removed immediately. Now I am not going to ask again. I am telling you all to SHUT THE HELL UP!"

The crowd quiets down to hear what the Sheriff has to say.

"Now, Travis and I were up by the ridge when everything went to hell. I don't have to tell you what's going on as you know what has been happening. What I need from everyone is to keep calm and to go home to be with your families-"

Sal Dickens interrupts the Sheriff once more. "Keep calm. Be with our families!-"

"Sal if you don't shut your mouth, I am going to throw your ass in jail! I don't want to hear another peep out of your mouth. Do you understand me?" The Sheriff gets right in the face of Sal Dickens. The town's folk become really quiet as Sal Dickens storms out of the grocery store. The Sheriff has had it with all the arguing going on in this time of crisis.

"You heard the Sheriff. Everyone just go home as we try to figure this all out. Now, come on get. You're better off being with your families then stuck here in this store." The Deputy escorts everyone out of the store as the Sheriff and the Mayor watch.

"I don't know what I would have done without you two, showing up when you did was perfect timing. It was getting pretty brutal in here." The Mayor walks over to the refrigerator grabs three beers from off the shelf handing the Sheriff and

the Deputy one. "What's going on out there Dale?"

"Well Charlie, it's like this. We are completely cut off from civilization.

That thing. Whatever it is. It just killed off the entire military. I mean. It swallowed

them whole and chewed them up."

Parker interjects. "It was mad. You should have seen it. It was a thick mist

sort of shit and all those screams then nothing. Like a void or something." The

Deputy takes a long drink of his beer. "What the hell is that now?!"

There is a different sound coming into the town square as the ground and

windows of the store start to shake. Loud engine sounds like a huge line of big rig

trucks rolling down a highway. The three men walk out to the street from the store

to see a line of military trucks coming up the street then stopping in front of them.

The door from one of the trucks opens as a military Captain gets out and walks over

to the Sheriff.

"Sheriff Higgins. I'm Captain Perry, United States Marines. Sir. You along

with these other gentleman have to come with us. I will explain later, but for now I

have orders and you must accompany me if you don't mind."

"With all due respect Captain. We aren't going anywhere. I have a town to

protect if you haven't noticed. So if you don't mind, I have work to do."

"Sheriff, your town is in lock down by the United States Armed Forces. We

have orders for you and your family to accompany me sir. You have no choice."

"Accompany you! Captain, look around you. Where are we going?" The

Sheriff starts to walk away from the Captain. Two military police stop the Sheriff in his tracks blocking him from leaving. The Sheriff turns and walks back to the Captain. "Ok! So now what?"

"Now will you come with me Sheriff. I'm sorry, but we have orders, which include you."

Deputy Parker looks at the Sheriff and smiles. "Well, well, well. Someone has just stepped up in this world. Looks like you're making friends fast there Dale."

The Sheriff grins at his Deputy. "I knew I hired the right guy to be my Partner. What do you think Travis? You up for a short ride with the US Military?" The Sheriff and the two men climb into the back of the military truck noticing there are others sitting in the darkness. The Sheriff hears a voice call his name from within the back of the truck as he takes his seat.

"Dale, thank God your safe!"

"Molly! You ok." The Sheriff hugs his wife and kids as he goes over to sit beside them. "What's going on here? Did they say anything to you at all?"

"No, nothing. I was outside with the kids when these trucks rolled up. They asked us to get in and that they were taking us to a safe place."

The Sheriff looks around at the faces looking back at him in the dark. "This should be interesting."

The trucks drive off with many of the town's folk within the back of the tarp covered cabs. The Sheriff and his family sit very quiet along with everyone else who are wondering where the military are taking them. It's a short ride through town as they finally come to a stop on one of the local farms just on the outskirts. The people are starting to climb out of the back of the trucks, while the tarp to the truck the

Sheriff and his family are riding in is pulled back allowing them to also climb out.

"The McKinnon Farm!?" The Sheriff looks around at all the town's folk as the military is massing them together in a tented camp area. The Sheriff watches the Captain walking over to where he and the others are standing. "Captain Gill, what is the meaning of this? Why are we on the McKinnon Farm?"

"It will all be explained in due time Sheriff. Now if I can get you and your Deputy to accompany me, Colonel Smith would like a word with you."

The Sheriff looks at his wife kissing her on the forehead. "Stay here with the kids, I will be right back." The Sheriff looks at the Captain very inquisitively wondering why the Colonel of the US Marines want to talk with him. "Ok Captain, lead on. This ought to be good."

The Sheriff and his Deputy are escorted to the Colonels tent, where plans are being made to accommodate the town's people. Father Murphy from the local church has been speaking with the Colonel most of the evening, they are preparing an initiative to cope with everyone they have rounded up.

"Colonel Sir. Sheriff Higgins and Deputy Parker as requested sir."

"Thank you Captain. Show them in."

Sheriff Higgins and Deputy Parker enter the Colonels briefing tent noticing all the radios and personnel milling about. The Sheriffs eyes become fixated on Father Murphy standing there waiting for them to walk over to speak with the Colonel.

"Come on in gentlemen, we don't have much time. I'm Colonel Smith and I am sure your acquainted with Father Murphy." The Colonel reaches over to one of

Time Shift – The Paradigm

his desks where much information is being placed about the phenomena happening.

The Sheriff looks at his Deputy then back to the Colonel. "What is the meaning of this Colonel? Why have you got my town on the McKinnon Farm?"

Father Murphy looks at the two standing there demanding an answer. "Dale, give the Colonel a moment to explain-."

"Father! Please. If you don't mind let's cut the shit. I haven't got time for your saving grace."

The Colonel sees the tension between the Sheriff and Father Murphy. He hands the Sheriff a photo taken by his intelligence. "Have a look at this for me. What do you make of that Sheriff?"

"I don't know. What is this?"

"Take a closer look. Look at the center of the photograph. What does that look like to you?"

The Sheriff looks closer at the photo. "What the hell is that! You got to be kidding me right?! Is this a joke Colonel?"

"No! It's no joke I assure you. What you see in that photograph isn't an illusion or a trick. That is the world as you see it."

The Sheriff looks at Deputy Parker who is totally stunned at what they are learning from this meeting. Deputy Parker speaks up as he does not believe what he is seeing.

"That! Whatever that is. What you're trying to say is, that is our world. That is a freaking science fiction movie. I'm sure I seen this on Television before." Deputy Parker hands back the photo to the Colonel.

Robbie Thomas

"Deputy Parker. That is no science fiction movie. That is your reality check son. Now I need the both of you to help me out in this mission. I need you two, to keep your town calm while we have everyone here on this farm. The reason you're here on this farm, is the fact the electrical impulses for some reason in this area are very low and it's the furthest from what is taking place out there."

"How do expect me to keep these people calm? Do you have any idea what you have just done? We have elderly and sick people out there-.

"Sheriff, one step at a time. We need you because they respond to you best. Now I have to get back to what I do, so I am counting on you." The Colonel looks up and over to his Captain. "Captain, take our Sheriff along with his Deputy back to their families. Oh and Sheriff. Let's not tell the others anything of what we talked about in here shall we. We don't need a panic on our hands, understand?"

The Sheriff turns to follow the Captain out of the tent when Father Murphy stops him for a brief moment.

"Dale, I would like to get everyone together to pray. Can I count on you to help me organize this?"

Sheriff Higgins squints his eyes trying to bite his tongue, but with everything coming to a head and earlier discussions with his wife about Father Murphy, he decides to speak up. He takes one step forward looking at Father Murphy in the eyes, pauses for a brief moment, and then slowly starts to express his feelings.

"Excuse me Father. I think we come from two different beliefs here. There's only two things in this world that will stop this madness. You my friend are not one of them. So if you don't mind, get the fuck out of my way, if you know what's good for you. All your praying and faith, where has it gotten us? Nowhere. Just look around you. If this is what praying and having faith is, I'm not buying it." The Sheriff turns and walks out of the tent as he is being escorted back to his family.

Travis can't believe his ears as what the Sheriff has just said. "Father I am really sorry for what the Sheriff just said. He had no right to speak to you that way."

"Don't worry son, we all have our own demons. Now go catch up with him he is going to need your help."

Parker runs to catch up to the Sheriff. "A little hard on the old fella there don't you think Dale?" Deputy Parker quite didn't like what happened between Father Murphy and his good friend Sheriff Higgins. "You have to give a little there partner; we're all in this together. I think you went too far speaking to Father Murphy the way you did, besides, a little respect goes a long way you know."

"Do me a favor Travis, stay out of it."

"You know no matter how you think of it or what you think you could have done back then Dale-."

"Don't go there Travis."

"I think it's time someone did Sheriff. There wasn't anything you could have done. It was either that kid or you."

The Sheriff grabs his Deputy's arm stopping in his tracks. "Travis, I don't ever want to talk about this again. I had a choice. I chose the wrong one. He was only a kid and I pulled the trigger. End of story. Now leave it alone."

"I just think you should stop beating yourself up about this Dale. That kid would have shot you dead in a blink of an eye. Father Murphy was right there when it all happened or do you forget that part."

"Your starting to piss me off Travis. I said leave it alone."

"You lost your faith Sheriff. I am your best friend and I have seen you change since then. You're not the same. You can't go on in life blaming something you had no control over."

"I had control over it damn it. I didn't have to pull the fucking trigger. I could have talked him down from that. I'm done with this conversation. Leave it the fuck alone. You hear me." The Sheriff walks away from the Deputy leaving him standing there looking at the Captain.

The Captain nods his head at the Deputy. "You're doing the right thing kid. Don't give up on him. A hard head like that needs someone close to him to break those bad thoughts. You're doing good."

"You think! He's a stubborn ass." The two start to walk back to the staging area where the town's folk are gathered.

The Sheriff walks back to his wife and children still waiting for him by the truck that brought them there. Payton, his son sees him coming and runs up to him jumping into his arms.

"Hey Payton pal! Love you son."

"Love you too daddy. Why are we all here with all these people?"

"It's just a small meeting son. We will all be going home real soon. Promise."

The Sheriff walks over to his wife. "Let's stay together and not wander off from one another. Jessica you hear me? Stay close to mom ok."

Robbie Thomas

Time Shift – The Paradigm

"Where am I going to go dad? I'm in the middle of a field on this farm."

Molly looks at the Sheriff with a worried look. "What did they say Dale? What are we all going to do?"

"They want all of us to be calm and stay put here for a while. I am sure we will be all able to go home real soon."

The Sheriff looks at his daughter Jessica asking her to sit by the truck with Payton. "Jessie, I need you to watch Payton here for a minute. Stay here and don't let him out of your sight." The Sheriff takes his wife off in the distance for a bit, away from prying ears so not to worry the kids with what he is about to tell her. "Mollie, they showed me a photo of that thing out there. It's more than just some mirage or mirror type image its alive."

"What is it Dale?"

"That photo was really screwed up. It was like looking into something that was on the other side of everything. It had our world in the photo. The funny thing about it, it wasn't our world. It couldn't have been. I mean, the planet I saw was dead, completely gone."

"Dale you're scaring me. What do you mean completely gone? We are all right here."

The Sheriff grabs his wife's arms and they kneel down looking around to make sure no one is listening. "The photo was like looking in a mirror at our world completely destroyed with no life on it." The Sheriff looks around again to see if anyone heard him. "What we need to do is get out of here as soon as we can."

"How Dale? They have everything blocked off. The military is everywhere."

Robbie Thomas

"Leave that up to me. I will get with Travis, we will think of something. But for now, we better get back. Don't tell anyone what I have told you ok. We don't want to create a panic."

The Sheriff and his wife make it back to the truck where Jessica and Payton are sitting waiting for them.

"Daddy!" Payton yells out as he runs up to him.

"Ok guys listen. We need to do whatever it is they ask of us. They are here to help and in a short while we will be going back home." The Sheriff kisses his son on the head and places him back on the ground. "Jessie, I need you to be the big sister. Help your mom out. Don't leave her side or Payton. I'm just going to go get Travis and I'll be right back."

The Sheriff looks around the mass of people that have gathered in the tented city the military has prepared for them. As he walks around he can hear the voices of many who call out to him wanting to know what is going on. He notices his Deputy standing talking with his wife and makes his way over to them.

"Travis, we need to talk. Hey Sam. This will only take a minute."

Travis looks at his wife Samantha, grabs her hand to ensure her everything will be ok. "I'll be right back. Don't worry; I'm sure the Sheriff has something figured out."

"What's up Dale?"

"Do you see what they are doing here? There is something about this area and what is going on. My best guess is they must have this under control to some degree."

Time Shift – The Paradigm

The Deputy looks around as military soldiers patrolling the perimeter are walking close to where they are talking. The two stop talking for a moment until the patrol is well passed them.

"I don't like what is going on here. I think we should get our families out of this mess and back to town." Dale leans towards Travis to speak keeping his voice down. "They have gathered us all here like cattle Travis. I do not like what I see."

While they are talking, Father Murphy slowly makes his way over to them. He observes the Sheriff and how anxious he seems.

"Good evening Travis and Dale."

"Good evening Father." Deputy Parker replies.

"I thought I would come over to express myself if I may. I want to explain; perhaps we got off on the wrong footing here this evening. I want to apologize for that."

"That's ok Father, I think Sheriff Higgins here is sorry too. Besides we have bigger things to work on here, right Sheriff?"

The Sheriff is hesitant to answer his Deputy but does. "You're right. Thanks Father for stopping by, I'm sure we will talk again."

"You're most welcome. You know it's not in how much a man feels in despair but how much he allows that despair to get to him. God Bless you two. Have a good evening." Father Murphy walks away as the Sheriff and the Deputy watch him go out of sight back to the gathering area.

"Man that guy gives me the creeps. I don't know what it is Travis but ever since-."

Robbie Thomas

Time Shift – The Paradigm

"Dude, you really have to lighten up about him. He was there that night it all went down; all he did was try to help. You have to remember he meant well."

"Maybe you're right! Maybe I should try to understand it more and stop putting the blame on others."

"I think you should stop putting the blame on yourself Dale. That is the biggest problem you have. You lost your faith man. Maybe through all this that is going on now, somehow it's a lesson for you, me and everyone."

"You might be right. I've never looked at it like that before."

"Perhaps it's time you did pal. I know you don't need this Dale, you're a good man."

The two men head back to where their families are, near the gathering area. As they are walking back, they are looking at the Phenomena that is lighting up the night sky. You can hear the billowing sounds of thunder in the distance. The air itself is filled with a thick mysterious instability that leaves a sense of something is about to take place at any moment. As they near the tented area, the Deputy notices the Sheriffs son off in the tree line standing talking into the darkness; however, there is a slight glow around him.

"Hey, isn't that Payton over there?"

"What the hell!?" The Sheriff starts to run over towards the area where his son is. "Payton. Son, get away from there." Both men finally reach where the Sheriff's son is standing.

"Payton. You ok? Let me look at you. What are you doing son?"

"Talking to the man Daddy."

Robbie Thomas

"What man Payton? There is no man here! Travis, check it out go that way. See if you see a man. Payton, where is this man?"

"He's gone now. He said he will come back again later."

"Payton. I don't see no man. What are you talking about?"

"He says we have to be nicer to each other and that a change is coming."

The Deputy comes back out of breath. "There's no one out there Dale."

"Payton. Who is this man you keep talking about?"

"He says we all have to have faith and pray more daddy! He comes from up there."

The Sheriff and the Deputy look at each other stunned to hear what Payton is talking about. The Sheriff grabs his son in his arms and they walk slowly away from the area where Payton was standing. There isn't a word spoken as the two men make their way back to camp.

"There he is! Where did you get off to Payton? You put a fright into mommy."

"I was talking to the man mommy."

"What's he talking about Dale?" Molly looks at the Sheriff inquisitively. "What man? Where?"

"Travis and I were talking when we saw Payton over by the tree line. There was this glow around him Molly. I can't explain it. It was like a glow of some sort. Anyways, he keeps saying he is talking to this man. We checked all around that area and there wasn't a man anywhere to be found. Travis went through the tree line, into the bushes back there and absolutely nothing. Not a sign of anyone."

Robbie Thomas

Molly kneels down with a smile holding her son. "Payton. Can you tell mommy who this man is? Is this the same man who comes to your room at home?

"Yes mommy. He says we have to pray more."

"Pray for what Payton?"

"He says there is a change coming. We have to be nicer to each other."

"Where is this man Payton?"

"He comes from the other side."

Molly looks up at both the Sheriff and the Deputy with a serious tone. "The other side, where Payton?"

There is pause as everyone is waiting for Payton to explain where this man comes from.

"He comes from over there." Payton lifts his head up pointing in the direction of the mysterious phenomena in the distance. "He watches us!"

Devastation Ahead

The Captain and the professors are now making their way through the jungle back to base camp anxiously waiting to see what Fisher was taking about. Upon entering the camp area, it becomes very apparent what has happened. An enormous sink hole has swallowed the camp along with its occupants. The dust from the event is still settling as much of the aftermath is now coming into focus. The horrific sight of what use to be base camp leaves a hallowed feeling in everyone's stomach.

The earthquake that created the gigantic sink hole has seemingly claimed the life of Steven Avery, Jose and Miguel her assistants along with the two soldiers Baker and Taylor. The hole has encompassed much of the camp taking most of their supplies as well. The landscape is now changed, leaving in its wake much devastation as the others are now looking emptiness in the face. The unsettling feeling of helplessness fills everyone as none of them were prepared for an event such as what has just happened.

The jungles tall trees and surroundings have shifted tremendously or have fallen to the ground. The event has come to make its mark, leaving its calling card for what is much more to come.

"No, no, no, Steven. This can't be happening. " Screams Elizabeth Ross as she falls to her knees in disbelief.

Michael comforts Elizabeth as the others are shocked to see what is before them. "I am so sorry Elizabeth."

Elizabeth gets up from her knees and struggles to understand what has just happened. She tries to make her way over to the huge sink hole. "Steven, Jose,

Robbie Thomas

Time Shift – The Paradigm

Miguel. Where are you?"

Captain McGuire yells out to Michael. "Professor! Stop her, don't let her go there."

Michael runs after Elizabeth. "Elizabeth. Stop." He catches her hugging her tight looking at the devastation only meters away from where they stand. "Elizabeth, you don't want to go any closer, it's not safe. Come on lets go back where David is."

Elizabeth is completely upset to see the amount of destruction the event has caused to her base camp and the loss of life. "You're right. Oh my god Michael, what happened here? Where is everyone?"

Michael takes Elizabeth back to where David is standing with Captain McGuire. Everyone is trying to collect their thoughts of what to do next. As the sounds of the Jungle start to settle, much comes into focus for everyone to see as it is very apparent this was a very strong earthquake. Everyone is talking and looking around at the mess created trying to figure out their next move, when all of the sudden a faint voice can be heard.

Captain McGuire motions everyone to be quiet. "People...People, quiet for a minute. Listen."

David sees what the Captain is doing. "Shh. The Captain hears something. Michael, Elizabeth look."

Captain McGuire puts his hand up in the air as to signal for everyone to be quiet. "Did you hear that? People please. Listen."

Elizabeth anxiously looks around. "Hear what? What do you hear?"

Robbie Thomas

Time Shift – The Paradigm

"Just a minute, keep quiet. It sounds like it came from over there."

A very faint sound can be heard coming from the abyss of the gigantic sink hole. It is very shallow and faint, barely heard by everyone. The sound is a voice crying for help, a plea for someone to reach in to pull them from the depths of hell.

Elizabeth freaks out as she recognizes the voice. "Oh my god! Its Steven, he's alive. STEVEN!"

Captain McGuire looks at everyone standing there. "Ross you stay here, Wright keep her here, you understand." Captain McGuire puts down his weapon while taking off his military vest. "We don't need anyone else getting hurt or falling into that hole."

Michael agrees with Captain McGuire while holding Elizabeth. "Yes Captain. You're right. We will all just stay here and let you do your job." Michael looks at Elizabeth to calm her. "He's right Elizabeth, let him do what he's got to do. We can't interfere or someone else might end up getting hurt."

McGuire looks over at Sgt. Fisher. "Fisher, come with me, I'm going to need a hand."

The Captain and the Sgt. make their way towards the edge of the huge hole, but it's unsafe. The outer edges are weak and very well could give way at any moment. The two discuss a viable way to reach Steven.

Fisher reinforces the fact of the situation. "Captain, be careful. It looks unsafe by the edge. The entire area is really unstable sir. We shouldn't be taking chances like this."

McGuire looks around at the situation at hand and agrees with Sgt. Fisher.

Robbie Thomas

"Right, ok look...go see if there is any rope we can use to tie me off so we can get to him. We have no time to lose here Fisher."

"Roger that sir!" Sgt. Fisher immediately takes the order and acts on it.

"Ok, hold on, were coming. Don't move were getting some rope." Captain McGuire yells towards the hole. "Fisher, hurry up, we don't have much time!"

Fisher managed to find some rope and was able to tie it off on tree not far off. He races back to where Captain McGuire is standing getting ready to descend into the hole to help Steven.

"Ok sir, it's tied off to the tree over there. We have enough rope for you to be lowered down just enough to reach him."

McGuire grabs the rope from Fisher. "Good Job Fisher. Now, I'm going to walk myself over to the edge and lower myself down. You hang on tight and when I say pull you pull got it!"

Sgt. Fisher confirms with the Captain. "Yes sir, not to worry, just be careful."

McGuire, as he is tying the rope to himself looks up at Fisher then to the others standing in the distance watching. "I didn't come all this way to fall into some freaking hole and die Fisher. You just pull when I say pull. Also keep an eye on Ross. She might just bolt once I pull him up. We don't want all of us going over the edge, you know what I mean!"

Fisher looks over at the others who are watching intensely and looks at the Captain. "Roger that sir!"

McGuire finishes tying the rope to his waste and pulls on it to see if it's tied tight enough so it won't come loose. "Right! Here I go, have an eye!"

McGuire makes his way to the edge of the abyss that is now looking him straight in the face as he is trying to save Steven from his death. His heart is racing as he knows the entire area is a huge risk to be doing what he is about to attempt. The ground beneath his feet becomes very soft as he sinks into it with each step closer to the edge. The earthquake has taken the ground sifting it making it very dangerous. The sounds of the jungle have now dissipated, as the only thing Captain McGuire can hear is the pounding of his heart in fear of what he is about to do.

Each step closer to the edge becomes much more of a fright than what was first anticipated. The eerie feeling in the air has the ominous touch to it that at any moment the ground can open and swallow him up, weighs heavy on the Captains mind. The Captain looks back at Sgt. Fisher who is being very attentive to his actions while holding the rope that is the very life line between Sgt. Fisher's hands and that of which is tied to his waist. Many thoughts run through the Captains mind as he prepares to help save Steven from his death.

McGuire takes a deep breath while slowly moving closer to the edge. "Ok, I am only a few feet from the edge. I am coming Steven, just hang on. Fisher more rope, more rope!"

The faint voice becomes just that much more loudly as the Captains senses are now on high intensity. The anxiety is filling him making the Captain more nervous than when he first started out.

"Hurry, hurry please!" A cry comes from Steven as he barely hangs on for life.

Robbie Thomas

"Steven! Don't move. I am coming, try to remain calm." Captain McGuire yells back to the dark hole.

The faint voice once again sounds very weak as an uncertainty can be felt now by everyone listening in. "I can't hang on any longer. I am so tired. Help me please!"

Captain McGuire finally sees Steven hanging on to part of the cliff with one arm as the other has been torn from his body. Steven is barely clinging to consciousness and losing his strength with each moment passing. McGuire lies down on the ground overlooking the edge and starts to stretch out his hand. He is only inches away from Steven as he tries hard to grab him. The Captain can see in Steven's eyes that he has no more strength at all and at any moment could lose his grip falling to his death.

"I see you, just hang on buddy. I'm going to get you out of there. Just stay with me Steven, just hang on." Captain McGuire inches his way closer and more into the hole trying desperately to reach Steven. "Don't you let go you hear me! Hang on damn it!"

Steven looking directly at Captain McGuire gives him a slight smile with the approval that he had tried everything he could possible to save him. "I can't hang on any longer."

The Captain frantically reaches with his outstretched hand calling on Fisher to give him more rope. "More rope Fisher, more rope for fuck sakes!" Then the Captain once again pleads with Steven to hang on. "Steven, buddy just hang on I am almost there. Don't you let go on me you hear me."

Robbie Thomas

Time Shift – The Paradigm

Fisher desperately hanging on to the life line of Captain McGuire's yells back. "That's all the rope there is Captain, there is no more!"

Just as McGuire is inches away from grabbing Steven, Steven loses his grip and slips from his hold down into the abyss of the sink hole. All that could be heard echoing from the darkness is the scream of Steven falling deeper and deeper to his fate. Captain McGuire can't believe what he has just witnessed and buries his head into his arm cringing at the fact he was just inches away from saving Steven. A very deep feeling of despair has now taken over everyone as they all know what Captain McGuire has just witnessed.

McGuire becomes enraged within himself at the fact of the entire situation and what is unfolding before his very eyes. He takes a moment to collect himself and yells back to Sgt. Fisher to pull him from the sink hole. "Fisher, Fisher, pull me up."

As Captain McGuire is slowly being pulled back up, he is starring down the endless abyss where he just witnessed Steven vanish into. With a horrified look on his face he is finally pulled from the edge of darkness. Fisher rushes over to assist Captain McGuire as he lay on the ground just looking up in disbelief at what had just happened. Fisher further pulls the Captain from the edge and checks him over to make sure he is ok. After addressing the current circumstance with Sgt. Fisher, McGuire issues a couple orders then makes his way over to the Professors sitting off in the distance. After addressing the current circumstance with Sgt. Fisher, McGuire issues a couple orders then makes his way over to the Professors sitting off in the distance.

Robbie Thomas

McGuire looks at Fisher very intensely while looking at the others over his shoulder. He takes the rope off his waste throwing it to the ground. "Fisher, we need to get the hell out of here. I don't want to be here while this all goes to shit."

Fisher also agrees and wants to know the next move. "What do you suggest we do Captain?"

McGuire brushes himself off and gathers his thoughts. "Well since Baker is gone and he had the communications phone, all we have is the satellite link for your laptop you have in your pack. Fire it up, find a signal and send this message. Two men down. Baker and Taylor are missing. Camp took heavy casualties, looking for safer ground for rendezvous pick-up. Will notify safe location at thirteen hundred hours."

Sgt. Fisher acknowledges the order. "Yes sir, on it now!"

McGuire walks over to the three awaiting to hear what happened to Steven. Elizabeth is very distraught in hearing the news that Steven couldn't hold on and slipped to his death. Elizabeth is in rage with sadness of the look on Captain McGuire's face and he is holding her back from running to the sink hole. The other two professors are discouraged in what they have just witnessed of one of their colleagues in his last moments.

Elizabeth tries to come to terms of what just took place. "What happened Captain? What happened to Steven?"

"Professor, there was nothing I could do. I'm sorry. Folks, we must find safer ground. We have to double back and cross that ridge over there taking to the high ground."

Time Shift – The Paradigm

The Captain walks away to speak with Sgt. Fisher about the communications he is having with the satellite hook-up on the laptop. Michael and David console Elizabeth as they get ready to do as the Captain has suggested. Sgt. Fisher is attempting to reach high command through satellite link up through the laptop as commanded by Captain McGuire.

Michael while holding Elizabeth tries to give her some encouragement. "Elizabeth, I am sure the Captain tried real hard to save Steven. Now we have to think about us, he's right you know, it's not safe to stay here."

Crying in the arms of Michael, Elizabeth reminds everyone just how loved Steven and the others are. "They were all good people, Jose, Miguel and Steven. Good people you know. The best a girl like me could ever have assisting in many things we did together over the years. I just can't believe they are gone." Elizabeth lets out one loud scream in anger over the entire episode of what took place. She then agrees with what the Captain has said and looks to Michael and David. "Your right, we must save ourselves now, we are all we have now."

Michael and David both hug Elizabeth as David tells her how much she is appreciated. "That's my Elizabeth. I have always admired your tenacity and strength. So let's do what the Captain says, he is only trying to help."

Michael looks at Elizabeth and asks her to help with David. "Hey give this old guy a hand up will you. I think a Mac Truck hit him back there. He's going to need us to take good care of him now!"

David agrees and looks off in the distance to where the Captain suggested they were to be heading. "We better get going, I have a feeling the Captain is going

Time Shift – The Paradigm

to have us hiking up that ridge real soon. Best we get a head start and keep well ahead of them."

Captain McGuire is now looking at what is coming across the Satellite Laptop connection with Sgt. Fisher. He doesn't like what he is seeing. High command has just put them on alert for another happening to take place very soon.

Fisher relays the message as it comes across the link up. "Sir. Command wants us to move due East 10 clicks. We have an anomaly headed our way and should hit our area in 2 hours. They are informing us to move immediately sir."

Captain McGuire looks baffled at what Sgt. Fisher has just told him. "What anomaly Sgt.? Ask command to confirm anomaly, what are we facing here?"

Fisher relays a message back to high command asking for further instructions and what type of anomaly was headed their way. They both stand waiting for the response in eagerness as there is a brief pause between messages. Suddenly the message comes through in a high alert status.

Central Command relays a message to the Captain and gives him orders. "You are to move 10 clicks east seeking higher ground immediately. You have a tsunami that will hit your area within a two hour period that will engulf that entire region. You will be further contacted later as for future pick up rendezvous area drop point. This is an order."

McGuire looks at Sgt. Fisher as they both can't believe their eyes. "Ask for confirmation Sgt. One more time."

Michael walks over to where Captain McGuire and Sgt. Fisher are. "Ok gentlemen, what is our next move?"

Robbie Thomas

McGuire looks at Michael in a very serious tone. "Standby, we are waiting for confirmation from high command."

Sgt. Fisher reads once more what has been sent again as a second confirmation from high command. "Sir! You're going to want to see this. It's coming in now. It is a tidal wave. They have confirmed a tsunami sir!"

I think we better bust ass and move it Sgt. We have no time to lose now. Professor, we have to be up that mountainside in less than an hour and a half. Let's move it." Captain McGuire is now in full operational mode and has to protect those that are left.

All three standing there are now looking at what is coming across the screen of the Satellite hook up with the laptop. The image coming across is of a grid like picture showing a tsunami headed their way fast from the middle of the Ocean.

McGuire once again reiterates his orders. "Ok people, we got to move. Come on let's move it! Sgt. Head up hundred yards making sure things are clear; I'll take the three professors with me. We're going to be right behind you so don't slow down, keep moving."

Michael can't believe what he just seen on the screen and is now in panic mode. "Captain, we must get to higher ground, there is no way we are going to out run a tsunami. Especially one of this magnitude."

Captain McGuire starts redressing himself with his vest and grabbing his weapon. "We're not going to out run it Professor. We are going to outsmart it. Now I need full cooperation from everyone here. We need to move and move now!"

Michael looks a bit confused, wants more information from the Captain.

"How do you suppose we are going to do this? Can't they just land a helicopter near bye and get us out of here?"

"That's rather difficult at this time Professor, since the Air Craft Carrier has pulled out an hour ago. They are trying to out run this wave themselves. Were on our own! So now if you please, let's move our asses before we get wet!" Captain McGuire gathers up a final few things before joining the remaining three standing waiting for him. He hurries along then joins the professors. "Professors! You see that mountain about a mile away. The average person can run a mile in under 20 minutes. I'm not asking you to run that in that time, but I am asking you to move as fast as you can. We're not only going to be at the base of that mountain in that time, but were going to be half way up it as well. Now move, we don't have time to waste."

David looks to his colleagues, Michael and Elizabeth in fright. "Ok well what the hell are we standing here for? We better move it and move it now."

The team make their way through the Jungle in a hurried pace as now they are not only racing against a tsunami, but they are racing against time. The intense moment is now shrouded with great fear of them being swept away from the huge wave about to ravage the coast line. The question running through their minds is not one of can they make it, rather will they make it!

Robbie Thomas

The News!

Meanwhile, back in Washington, more bad news from around the world is coming into the President's Office at the White House. High level meetings with the Russians President are happening on the phone with the logistics coming through from Central Intelligence. The grim reality of other nations are now taking center stage as what use to be things you would read about in books or see on Sunday night movies, are now becoming the life of everyone around the world. Remarkable happenings are taking place in Russia, that has the United States Government a little worried as to where is this all headed and what is next.

The White House has activated many of its members of congress informing them of the situation and circumstances taking place. Individual States have proceeded to put Martial Law into effect calling out the National Guard, Coast Guard and Police Agencies to keep law and order along the West Coast. Preparations are well underway as Central Intelligence has indicated the forthcoming events to come through the alert system for all agencies.

The White House scrambles to gather all Intel and up to date information of any other anomalies taking place around the world. The anxiety is at a very high pitch as many decisions are now being made by the President of the United States and his team. Secretary of State Robert Sims enters into the Oval Office informing the President of an emergency phone call coming in from the Russian President, Nicolas Konstantin.

"Mr. President, we have President Konstantine from Russia on the emergency line sir. Their country is in total chaos. The Domensk Region is totally

Time Shift – The Paradigm

destroyed and now Moscow is about to fall."

President Samuel Morgan stops what he is doing to look at Secretary of State

Robert Sims in a serious tone. He then looks to the rest of his committee patiently

waiting for the President to pick up the phone. The President slowly picks up the

Red phone to the right of his desk. "President Konstantine. This is President

Morgan, is there anything we can do to assist you?"

The Russian President with a nervous tone to his voice slowly replies his

message to the President of the United States. "Not much one can do now Mr.

President. The worlds fate is in the hands of whatever this is that is coming for us

all. My beloved Russia has been taken, my country is no more. We are at a time of

great despair, there is nothing you nor the world can do now."

President Morgan pauses as he hears the fear in the voice of what use to be

his biggest adversary. "Surely there must be something we can do to help you Mr.

President. You must get out of there. We can assist you in this way."

President Konstantine goes silent for a moment. You can hear a pin drop in

the Oval Office as all eyes are on President Morgan. The proud deep voice of

President Konstantine relays his thoughts back to President Morgan. "There is

nowhere to go my friend. There is nowhere to hide from this Phenomenon. My

beloved Russia is no more as my people are dying by the thousands. Cities and

villages are being engulfed by this thing, this…this happening."

President Morgan stands up from his chair at the Oval Office Desk. "Nicolas,

there has to be a way. You must get out of there!" President Morgan motions for

Secretary of State Robert Sims to approach the Desk. "Nicolas, let the United States

Robbie Thomas

Time Shift – The Paradigm

help you."

The sounds of off in the distance thunderous rumblings can be heard over the phone in the Russian President's office as President Morgan listens very intensely. The horrible feeling that is now running through the President sends a deep feeling of helplessness to his very soul. As both Presidents are talking on the phone, President Konstantine is looking out his office window starring fate in the face as a wall of fire is now engulfing Moscow. The raging noise is terrifying as President Morgan can hear what Nicolas is seeing on the other end.

President Konstantine stands up out of his chair looking out the window of his office. "No I am sorry, there is nothing we can do. Save yourself if you can. Goodbye my friend!"

The President is now looking at his staff in horror as he hears the very end of the Russian President and Russia itself. The phone is sharply disconnected with a loud thunderous rumble. Everyone in the Oval Office is quiet as they are now just looking at the President of the United States. "Mr. Sims we need to issue a warning to the people of the United States. I need to be on television informing them of what is going on."

Secretary of State Robert Sims looks at the President and immediately agrees. "Yes sir! Right away Mr. President. I will get the press room ready." Robert Sims walks towards the door of the Oval Office stops then turns to speak to the President. "Should I include all news agencies, or just the ones on the emergency list?"

President Morgan thinks for a moment as he wants to get the word out to the

Robbie Thomas

nation. "Yes you better include the secondary list as well Mr. Sims. We don't want to leave out anyone. They just might write something, or televise their own version creating more havoc than what there is already."

Robert Sims smiles softly. "You're right, will do sir!"

The President looks to Vice President Donald Reise. "Donald, have we heard back from Admiral Johnston, from the Roosevelt?"

"Not of late. The last we have is he pulled out from the coast of Peru trying to out run the Tsunami. They gave a timeline of approximately one hour to maneuver away from the event."

The President walks to the middle of the Oval Office. "Good! Establish communication with the Admiral and get me his position. I want to know if our ships are out of harm's way."

The Secretary to the President walks into the Oval Office with disturbing news for the President. The tension in the White House is now at a very feverish pitch. Martin Wedeman is a very conservative political right hand of the President. He has now come with news from the National Guard in California.

"Mr. President. We have breaking news out of California. They just had an earthquake sir. It measured 9.0 on the Richter Scale. There is much damage to the core of Los Angeles and the quake traveled the fault line to San Francisco which took a huge hit."

Martin Wedeman turns on the Oval Office Television as the news is playing out of the destruction in Los Angeles and San Francisco.

New Reporter Sandra Goodman is reporting live from the devastation in Los

Angeles. "Live from channel 11 news in Los Angeles. What we just experienced is a magnitude earthquake of 9.0 on the Richter Scale. As you can see much of the metropolis is in ruins from this large quake that lasted for more than 3 minutes. A secondary quake happened just moments after the initial one and it too was a very strong one at 8.0. There are people dead in the streets as panic has now set in. Everywhere you look there is so much damage, so much death and destruction, Los Angeles is in ruins. If you're inside a building you have to get clear of the structure for it will not be safe. Get out in the open, away from immediate buildings. Emergency crews and Police are on their way, stay calm. Again, Los Angeles has been hit by a 9.0 magnitude earthquake! If you are in need of assistance seek out help immediately, this is Sandra Goodman CYN Channel 11 news Los Angeles."

Vice President Donald Reise looks immediately at the President. "Sam, you're wife. She was at the gala for the Governor in Los Angeles tonight."

The President walks back around his desk to take a seat and grab the phone. "Mr. Wedeman try and get my wife on the phone, try and get someone on the phone immediately. Mr. Wedeman, I want to know if she is ok, do whatever you need to do."

Martin Wedeman leaves the Oval Office to locate the President's Wife and family. The tension in the White House is now on high and the alert level is the highest ever as the world is in total chaos. The White House Chief of Staff now enters into the Oval Office informing the President that the press room is ready for him. The camera crews from all the news agencies are ready to telecast the President's address to the People of the United States.

Robbie Thomas

Time Shift – The Paradigm

Anne Reynolds who is the White House Chief of Staff enters into the Oval Office. "Mr. President, we are ready for you to address the people of the United States sir."

The President looks at Anne Reynolds. "Yes. Ok thank you Ms. Reynolds. Well gentlemen. Let's inform our nation shall we."

The President sits behind his desk in the Oval Office pauses for a moment of reflection collecting his thoughts. He stands and buttons his suit jacket, straightens his tie and slowly looks at each individual in the room. He then makes his way to the Oval Office door, immediately making his way for the press room. He is walking speaking with the Vice President and the White House Chief of Staff as they enter the press room. He approaches the podium as all eyes from the press are on him. Every camera in the room are now focused on the President of the Unite States. The silence is deafening and the tension is high. The president will now address the nation.

President Morgan looks around the room at the news teams and reporters anxiously awaiting his address. "People of the United States, this is your President. I know I don't have to explain to you what is going on around the world. For the most part, it is on every news channel on television. What I will tell you and I am being forth coming here. The world is in a grave situation at present. This phenomena event that is transpiring worldwide is devastating every country as we know. We here in Washington are working hard to find out what it is that we are up against. We encourage you to stay safe in your homes with families or to seek shelter until this is over. Please keep calm while we are working on this situation. We will work this out. May God Bless and keep all of you Safe and God Bless America."

The President is immediately escorted out of the Press Room as you can hear the reporters asking questions that go unanswered. The President is accompanied by his staff as they make their way back to the Oval Office. The White House is now a buzz with activity on all levels as calls from around the world and the leaders of other nations are filtering through to the Presidents Staff members. The President enters into the Oval Office and is met by the Secretary of State Robert Sims who is waiting news from the Roosevelt.

Meanwhile the USS Roosevelt is steaming along as the tsunami is about to strike. They have failed to get out of harm's way. The Tsunami is just too large in size and to vast in its stretch throughout the Pacific Ocean. The men on board are now bracing for the impact about to take place. Captain Davis along with his crew are on deck as they are witnessing this two hundred plus foot high wall of solid water roaring down on them. The horror on their faces says it all.

"What is your fondest memory Daniels out of all the years' service you have given aboard this ship" Captain Davis walks over to the radar to see the positioning of the USS Roosevelt. "I mean if there was one thing that stands out in your mind son, what would that one thing be"

Officer Peter Daniels stands silent for a moment before answering the Captain. "I guess it would be the day they assigned me to the crew sir. I have always wanted to serve under your direction and I thank you for everything."

Captain Davis smiles while walking back over to Officer Daniels to shakes his hand. "Well Daniels, it's been a pleasure. Believe me it truly has. When your father and I served in the first Gulf War together, he always thought you would grow up and serve well in the Navy. It was his dream for you." Captain Davis looks at Daniels smiling knowing his father would be very proud of him.

Officer Daniels stands fast listening to the old stories Captain Davis is sharing with him. "Yes sir, he always told me I would make a good sailor one day either that or a great shoes salesman." Daniels laughs at the latter part of his comment for that is exactly what his father did say to him.

Captain Davis grins putting his hand on Officer Daniels shoulder. 'Yes indeed you got that right Daniels. Your father was a great man. We all can learn something from his legacy that is for sure."

"OH MY GOD! Captain off the starboard bow." Officer Daniels sees the thick black wall of water bearing down on them. "Sound the Alarm!"

Captain Davis looks at what Officer Daniels just screamed out. "Sound the alarm, brace for impact! Turn her about, nose into this."

Second in command Russ Waters is frozen in fear of what he sees. "Captain we don't have time! Brace for impact!"

The sound of the Ocean bearing down on the USS Roosevelt is horrifying. As the solid wall of water roars towards the air craft carrier, the sound of death encompasses them. Everyone on board all vessels are now scrambling in fear as this monster has its sights set on them. The mass of water slams into the ships as the sound of twisted metal echoes the huge wall of water. It consumes everything in its path leaving nothing in its wake. The horrific moments aboard the vessels are now met by the quiet sounds of the deep. The Ocean has come claiming its victims swallowing everything in its path.

Back at Navel Headquarters the last message received was one of horror. Navel Petty Officer T. Jones who received the message can't believe what he just heard as he sits numb as the final broadcast was intercepted by his radio. Alongside Navel Petty Officer T. Jones in the communications room is Staff Sgt. Kennedy, who watches in horror on the radar what once was blips of ships disappear right before his eyes.

Navel Petty Officer T. Jones can't believe what he has just heard or is seeing. "Holy shit, this can't be happening! Sgt. We have to get this message to the Admiral's Office ASAP!"

Staff Sgt. Kennedy is also stunned at the event that just took place. "What the hell just happened Jones!? Send a message to search and rescue immediately. Stay posted and contact me immediately if anything happens. I am on my way to the Admiral's Office."

"Yes sir!" Petty Officer Jones watches intensely to see if anything at all comes up on radar or if anything transmits over the radio as Sgt Kennedy races out of the communications room.

News has now reached the high command of the Navy and a message has been sent back to the White House, where they wait the fate of the USS Roosevelt. As the President and his team are working hard in the Oval Office making calls to other leaders around the world as a staff member of Secretary Of State Robert Sims passes the long awaited message to him.

Secretary of State Robert Sims acknowledges his personal aid as she enters the Oval Office with the message he has been waiting for. "Ah, yes Sally. Did we hear anything from the Admirals Office as of yet?" Robert Sims is passed a note from his personal aid and reads it. He looks to the President in shock as everyone in the room has gone silent waiting to hear the news. "Sir, this comes directly from the Admiral himself."

President Morgan feels something is terribly wrong with the tone Robert Sims has just used. "What is it Robert? Out with it."

Robert Sims looks around the room with a heavy heart and announces the demise of the USS Roosevelt. "I have bad news. The Roosevelt was unable to outrun the tsunami that was in the Pacific Sir. We lost contact with her and the destroyers accompanying her."

The President looks at the sinking feeling in the room in everyone's eyes as the news was just told from Robert Sims. "Well, what do you say to that!?" The President pauses for a moment while looking at Robert Sims. "God Bless those men and women! Those brave men and women on those ships." The President within the silence of the room sits at his desk, puts his hands on his head as he looks down. In his brief moment of silent prayer, he lifts his head up looking once again at every single soul standing in the Oval Office awaiting his words. "Alright, let's not just stand there staring at me. Let's not let their lives be in vain. We have much work ahead of us. We have a nation looking to us to solve this problem and DAMN IT, I'm not going to sit here letting this thing win. I want every report possible from every source we have at our disposal on my desk in a half hour. Move it people, I want answers and a solution now!"

Robbie Thomas

Time Shift – The Paradigm

Robert Sims grabs paper work from the President's desk. "Absolutely, right away sir!" Robert turns to his personal aid. "Sally I want data from SATCOM immediately on what is going on in Peru, Russia and Europe." Robert Sims and his aid leave the Oval Office in a hurry discussing the next steps they are going to take for the President.

Vice President Donald Reise walks over to the President at his desk. "Sam, I am heading back to my office to make calls to Canada and General Wilcox in the Philippines-.

The Vice President and President are interrupted by White House Chief of Staff Anne Reynolds. "Sir. This is just breaking on the news now!" Anne Reynolds once again turns on the Oval Office television to see the breaking news. "They are broadcasting from the heart of Los Angeles Sir, with an update!"
The entro to the news station is just playing and coming on air. "CYN Channel 11 News where breaking news comes first." The news anchor is being handed the breaking news while the cameras are rolling live. "Good evening I am Brad Wilson and welcome to CYN Channel 11 News. We are just getting in at this moment breaking news from Los Angeles, where Sandra Goodman has been covering the latest. Sandra are you there?"

The camera shot changes now as live coverage from the middle of Los Angeles is being televised of the devastation from the 9.0 earthquake. "Yes Brad, we are in the heart of Los Angeles where it seems the most damage was done. As you can see, most of what use to be the core of Los Angeles is in vast ruins now. There are many people in the streets hurt from the falling buildings and death is

Robbie Thomas

everywhere. We are actually at the Governors function, where the First Lady was to attend, however, what was the International Hotel where this was to take place is completely gone."

The sound of sirens screaming past the News team interrupts them as they are trying to make their way through all the rubble. The news team manage to notice a few people climbing out of the fallen building of the hotel and run over to assist. "Tommy, Tommy, follow me, look there are people coming out." Sandra Goodman runs over to help a couple coming out from the rubble and who are hurt badly. "Are you ok? Here sit here. Tommy put the camera down and help me." Sandra tears part of her jacket she is wearing to wipe away some of the blood off the face of the woman she is attending to. "Don't move, let me help you."

The lady from the Hotel is crying and shocked at what has happened. "They're all dead! Oh my god, someone please help them."

Sandra Goodman still attending to the woman asks her about the First Lady and the Governor. "Do you know if anyone at all is still alive in there? Did you see the First Lady and the Governor, are they alive, do you know?" Sandra looks at Tommy who is still filming as everything is happening. She turns once more to the woman who is in shock asking her to recall if the First Lady was ok. "Ma'am, ma'am, do you know if the First Lady is ok?"

The woman, Sandra is helping, lets out a cry that is of ill feeling as she looks right at the news woman. "No, no one made it out of there. Everyone is gone!"

Sandra looks at Tommy her camera man telling him to cut filming. "Tommy CUT, this is Sandra Goodman CYN Channel 11 News. Back to you Brad." Tommy stops filming and the broadcast goes dark.

Back at broadcast central everyone is stunned from what they just seen from Sandra Goodman. Brad Wilson tries his best to recover from what was just broadcasted. "Um, we thank you Sandra for that. Folks, we are in a time of sadness as we just learned about the First Lady and the Governor of California. I don't know what to say, this is terrible indeed. I am Brad Wilson, and this is breaking news at CYN Channel 11 Los Angeles, we will be back right after this."

The news broadcast goes directly to commercial as the nation has now just learned the fate of the First Lady. No one more shocked or stunned than the President of the United States. His heart has just fallen, with the news of his wife not surviving the earthquake. Everyone in the Oval office is stunned. Not a word is spoken. All eyes are on the President as the silence becomes deafening.

Vice President Reise tries to comfort the President. "Sam, oh my god, Sam I am sorry."

President Morgan just raises his hand, to indicate no one say a word as he walks over to the picture of his wife on his desk. He stumbles as he can't believe what he has just heard. Time just seems to have stopped, while everyone in the room is feeling the despair the President has right now. He picks up the picture of the First Lady and lovingly touches her face in the photo while a tear slowly rolls down his face. "She was my best friend. The love of my life." There is a pause and no one is saying a word. The President lets out a scream that came from the depths of his soul. "God why? I love her so much. You can't do this to me!" The President's staff is all heartbroken as they too can not believe what has just happened. The President holds the picture of his wife to his chest, close to his heart as tears stream down his face.

The unknown is making itself known completely around the world taking whatever

it wants leaving nothing behind. Deaths door has opened, claiming many in its

wake. The despair and empty feeling of helplessness is felt worldwide. This is but a

dream, a nightmare as the horror is consuming the very being of mankind.

Robbie Thomas

Taking to Higher Ground

Captain McGuire and the Professors make their way through the Jungle to the mountain as they are now facing the tsunami making its way to where they are. The trek is a big of one as they have to compensate for Professor Gates injuries along the way. The Jungle is unforgiving, which is hampering progress for them making it to their destination before they are met with the tsunami bearing down on them.

They notice the sounds of the Jungle have now changed with the silent nothingness that surrounds them. The inhabitants, which normally kept the Jungle alive with vigour, have now ceased as if they have disappeared altogether. Not a bird or animal can be seen or heard anywhere. The strangeness in the air is overwhelming to the team as they are taking notice of all the changes that are occurring around them.

"Come on Professors, keep up, we don't have time to waste." Captain McGuire is looking around and into the trees for any sign of activity of animals. "Fisher, have you noticed the sounds or any movement in the Jungle at all?"

"I thought something seemed a bit different," Fisher looks around, noticing the quietness coming from the Jungle. "It's awfully quit Sir!"

"Don't you worry about us, Captain. You just keep going were right behind you." Michael yells ahead as he slowly makes his way with David and Elizabeth. "We will keep up, don't you worry." Michael is helping David along the way and remarks about the captain to his colleagues. "Charming fellow, that Captain is." The three laugh at the funny comment Michael has just made.

Robbie Thomas

David isn't feeling the best and is starting to slow them down. "I have to stop for a minute have to catch my breath."

Elizabeth looks at her poor esteemed colleague and agrees. "Yes, we will stop for a moment to catch our breath. That Captain will just have to wait for us is all."

"What the hell do you think you're doing? Do you realize at all what we are facing?" Captain McGuire checks his watch. "You stop now that wall of water is going to take you with it. I suggest you get up and move it right away."

"Look Captain we are not in your Army. We are human. We are going to take a small break if you like it or not. Another thing! Your disposition is not becoming of you." Elizabeth snaps at McGuire. "Can't you see David is in need of some rest? Now, I suggest to you, unless you want to carry him on your shoulders, I would allow brief breaks for all of us to rest."

McGuire looks at the three of them and seeing that David is not in the best of shape agrees with Elizabeth. "Alright, two minutes. Two minutes that's all you get."

Elizabeth smiles and in her charming way looks at McGuire. "Yes Sir, Captain Sir! You're such a humanitarian."

McGuire just looks at Elizabeth, turns and walks back to where Sgt. Fisher is standing. "I think that Professor Ross is going to be trouble Fisher, I just have my feelings on this."

"Well she has been in this Jungle for some time now Captain. The sun or something must be getting at her." Fisher starts to laugh.

"Yah right! It's something alright! Ok, while we take out 2 minute break,

Time Shift – The Paradigm

upload the link to the satellite; get me info on the tsunami." McGuire while waiting

for the information to come through on the laptop fisher using he yells to the three

sitting in the distance. "Ok folks! We move our asses in two. I am waiting for Sgt.

Fisher to get me info on that tsunami heading our way. Once hc has that we move.

Got it?"

Michael looks back motioning with his hand that he hears the Captain. "Yes

thank you Captain." then mumbles to Elizabeth and David. "He is going to run us

ragged I tell you. David, how are you feeling?"

"I am fine, just a couple more minutes if we can. I should be good then."

Sgt. Fisher has just downloaded the latest Intel information from central

command. The tsunami is about an hour away from making landfall and gaining

speed. McGuire sees the latest information and starts to figure out another plan to

get everyone to safety as soon as possible. Looking at what he is faced with and the

surroundings that are in front of him the logistics and timing of the tsunami will

leave them very little time to spare in reaching their objective.

Fisher looks at the Captain knowing very well they will be cutting it very

close in getting to the Mountain. "It doesn't look good does it? Do you think we will

make it in time?"

McGuire deep in thought looks at Fisher with concern on his mind. "We are

going to make it. How we make it up that Mountain is another thing but we are

going to make it!"

Just as McGuire and Fisher are talking about their tactics in getting to the

Mountain another message comes through over the satellite hookup to the laptop.

Robbie Thomas

Time Shift – The Paradigm

Fisher starts to relay the message to McGuire standing there. "Sir, another message coming in from central command. It reads. 'Tsunami has over run the Roosevelt and its crew. Tsunami is roughly one hour from making landfall. Find higher ground immediately.' Shit!" Fisher can't believe what he is reading and closes the laptop.

McGuire also can't believe what he has just been told in the message. "Shit! Ok, look. We have to keep these three moving and we must get our asses up that mountain. You just keep moving twenty meters ahead of us clearing a path. I'll keep them moving."

Fisher packs up the laptop grabs his weapon and begins to move out. "Roger that Sir! On my way."

McGuire makes his way over to the professors resting to give them the news. "Ok, now I want you three to listen to me and listen good. We just got Intel in that puts us at a very vulnerable possibility of being hit by this tsunami sooner than we think. I strongly suggest we move and move now. No more breaks until we are upside that mountain."

"Is it that bad Captain?" Elizabeth asks as she stands up.

"Ma'am, it's worse than we thought so I suggest we just keep moving and fast."

The team have made it through the Jungle at a hurried pace, making it to the base of the Mountain. The worry among them is still very real and intense as everything seems different in the air. The Captain and the three professors struggled up the side of the mountain to get more than 300 feet up. They are making good time in doing so but as they get higher up, they are again met with an aftershock that are

Robbie Thomas

small but still hinders their climb. Rocks from ledges above them are now falling causing them to stop and take cover. Everything that can go wrong is but they are still striving to make it up the side of the Mountain. The climb is a tedious one with many dangers however, with the persistence of Captain McGuire pushing the Professors they are making good time and to a safe level.

There is a loud roar starting to come from the distance as dust and debris can be seen as if something just took the ground below and shook it. The ugliness of a monster is now rearing its head, engulfing the jungle floor tearing everything in its path to shreds, swallowing it whole. The sickening sounds of complete trees being snapped in half as well as the being uprooted from their base is becoming louder and louder as this tsunami rages through jungle. They are now out of dangers path however as they can see the devastation the large wave is doing.

Michael just stares at the wall of water making its way towards them. "It's huge! Look how it's destroying everything in its path."

"Sir! I found a Plateau just up ahead" Sgt. Fisher yells over the deafening sound of the wave. "No more than ten meters up, come on!"

"Ok folks you heard him, let's get up there then we can rest" McGuire leans down to help David up on his feet. "Here grab hold!"

David grabs McGuire's Hand. "Thanks, I mean that! If you didn't push us Captain, we would still be down there in that mess" David looks at the ravaging wave taking everything it can is its path.

"It's my job Professor. Just doing my job."

The five make it to the plateau area which is now going to be their camp site for the night. It's a safe area large enough they will be well away from the edge of the mountain. They get up to the plateau and start to realize it's just not a plateau but something seems mysterious about this area. The three professors start to take a closer look.

Captain McGuire puts his weapon and packing down on the ground. "Alright, this is where we will set up camp for the night. It's a safe as we are going to be for the time being.

"How long before someone comes to get us, Captain?" David asks as he takes a seat on large rock.

"That I don't know Professor but as soon as Fisher sets up, he will hook up to the satellite then we should know from command."

"Glad we all got up here, thanks Captain. I know we might seem like a pain in the ass to you, but I assure you we mean well for a few old geeks." Elizabeth jokingly remarks.

McGuire smiles at Elizabeth and welcomes her fun sarcasm. "Professor it wouldn't be an adventure if we didn't have some excitement now would it." McGuire turns to Fisher asking for the satellite hookup to be initiated. "Fisher as soon as you set up, get me command on the hook up."

"Michael, look at the way this area is shaped. David, do you see what I see? This is so reminiscent of a meeting area or a platform not plateau." Elizabeth is making her observations of the area looking at the structure of the landing. She notices certain intricacies that resemble something more than just a plateau on the side of a mountain.

Robbie Thomas

"Your right it does look similar doesn't it? Look at the position of those rocks on the wall. You don't think it could be-.

Michael is interrupted by a very excited Elizabeth as she now is becoming aware of this area and what it is. "Michael help me. Come here. The over growth help me pull on it." Elizabeth begins to pull vigorously on the vines and overgrowth on the wall.

McGuire looks up at what Elizabeth is doing. "Hey, hey! What do you think you're doing? You're going to cause rocks to come down on us." McGuire gets up, runs over to where Elizabeth is now pulling on the overgrowth trying to make her stop. "Don't do that unless you want rocks to come down on us, are you crazy?!"

"Captain, do you know anything about archaeological finds." Elizabeth continues to move the growth away from what she suspects is an opening in the wall in front of her. "No Captain. See it's only attached here running along the side of the structure here. These are vines grown up from the ground not from above. Come on help pull."

As the three of them are pulling on the foliage around what seems to be an opening of some sort in the side of the mountain, Professor Gates is sitting beside Sgt. Fisher and they both get a better look at what is taking place. As the vines are coming down etchings in the rocks above the opening appear and other markings. Professor Gates and Sgt. Fisher are stunned to see this unfold before their eyes.

Elizabeth steps back to take a better look at what they have uncovered. "Michael, Michael look! I just knew it. It's an opening."

"Look at the rocks above the opening Elizabeth, they have markings!"

Michael is excited and continues to move the over growth away to get a better look at what is etched in the stone above. "Look at the markings here and here!"

While the two professors are clearing the overgrowth from the wall of the new opening they have just discovered, Captain McGuire decides to walk over to Sgt. Fisher to see if he has established communication with Central Command.

"Fisher, how's our link with command going?

"Well from NASA data the wave hit the entire coastline of Peru. Command says to stay put until E-Vac arrives. They don't know how long that will be but told us to remain at these coordinates." Fisher shows McGuire what is coming across the satellite hookup.

"Get back on that thing and stress we need timeline" McGuire pulls out a map of the area and starts logging data points for sinking up with E-Vac. "Tell them we are-"

Fisher interrupts the Captain. "Sorry sir command says no timeline available. We are to remain at position keeping communication lines open."

Captain McGuire looks exhausted from receiving that last message and gives in to what is now their new campsite. "Ok well I think this is going to be home for a bit folks. Better batten down and get use to it, it looks like we will be here for a while."

Michael walks over to McGuire. "Come on Captain. Where is your sense of adventure? Let's make the most of it while we can. Now do you have a flashlight in all that gear you have."

McGuire just grins and reaches for a flashlight handing it to the Professor.

"Careful now, don't go wasting all the juice in that. I don't know how much we have left in the batteries." McGuire looks at Fisher like he isn't impressed at all. "Tell me this is not happening. This is not happening to me."

David is excited to see the new find Elizabeth has uncovered stands up slowly putting his hand out to the Captain. "Surely, you can't tell me you're not at least a little interested in knowing what's in there Captain. This is where the adventure begins."

"My adventure is remaining safe right here and now. We are to remain here until the E-vac team arrives. Look around you Professor. I think my attention is on what is going on out there. I suggest you three stay put and do what we're doing." McGuire is very adamant in what he is saying knowing that leaving the area would risk them being rescued.

Sgt. Fisher speaks up as a new message is coming into Captain McGuire from central command. The professors walk over with the Captain to see what is coming over the satellite hookup.

"Captain, I think you want to see this!" Fisher takes a serious tone.

David and Michael are now both looking at what is being transmitted over the laptop.

David leans in putting his glasses on. "What the hell is that?"

"That Professor is LA, wiped out. That is the entire core of Los Angeles devastated from an earthquake. That is what that is."

Fisher is now receiving more data coming in. "Sir there is more. This is photo link to Russia which NASA is sending now. It's coming in slow." Fisher expands the screen to get a better look at what is being sent them. "Damn! Would you look at that, holy shit?"

The five of them are now looking at the satellite view of the destruction in Russia that has taken place. The overview shows much of the landscape changed from the Phenomena Event taking place there. The regions in Russia are forever changed as complete cities and villages have been consumed like a flesh eating disease, taking everything it has in its sights.

Elizabeth can't believe her eyes as she is being held by David. "What the hell is going on. What could possibly have done that."

The satellite link goes dark. Transmission has stopped and signal is lost. "That's it Sir. We lost signal. Doesn't look like we're going to be able to regain it anytime soon either." Fisher closes the laptop sits back reflecting on what he has just witnessed.

"Ok people. You saw what I saw. Now I strongly suggest we stick to the plan and wait for E-vac. No wandering off or getting lost in some damn cave." McGuire as well can't believe what he has just seen from all the information Central Command has transmitted to them. "With the Satellite down now and with no further communications coming through, I suggest we stay put."

This is not sitting well with David and he is starting to get a little irate with everything going on. "I want to know what the hell Washington is doing to get us out of here! I didn't sign on to this at all. I am a fucking professor, not military issue G.I. Joe shit!"

"I for one am not going to sit around when no one is coming for us. I don't know about you Captain McGuire, but I plan on getting off this rock as soon as I find a way." Michael takes a bold stance not liking at all the circumstances they have been dealt. "I am with David! You better come up with something-.

McGuire stands up quickly and right in Michaels face. "Something or what?! What are you suggesting my dear Professor? What are you going to do about it?" McGuire pushes Michael away from him. "Don't you think for one fucking moment I don't want out of this mess that we are all in. Don't you dare go there Professor, you're barking up the wrong tree fella."

David doesn't like what McGuire is doing to Michael and makes it known. "You're telling us they're sending a search party, when all this shit is going on around the world. Who do you think we are?"

"Listen to me and listen good-". McGuire tries to speak but again is interrupted.

"No you listen! I have given enough time doing what you want and it has gotten us nowhere. In fact it has gotten us in such a mess look around you, what are we going to do?

McGuire has just about had it with the Professors and their complaining. "I'll tell you what I am going to do." McGuire reaches for his sidearm and about to pull it out.

Fisher stops McGuire from losing control. "No don't." Fisher then looks at David and Michael. "I think its best you two back off and stand down if you know what's good for you."

"Let me tell you something professor! There's absolutely no where to go! I am not your babysitter and if you feel you can find a way to get us out of here, I am

for it. But I know you wouldn't be able to find your ass from a hole in the ground. So

if I were you, I would shut the fuck up and do as your told. All you're going to do is

end up killing yourself and maybe us too so sit your ass down and let me do my

work." McGuire walks away from the two professors to calm himself down.

Elizabeth jumps in on the bravado going on with the men. "Everyone just

shut up for a minute and hear me out. We can sit here doing nothing arguing or we

can try to find another way. Now I know this might sound a bit crazy but I think we

might find a way through that opening. There is absolutely no other way off this

rock so I suggest perhaps we try another alternative way."

David agrees with Elizabeth. "I'm with her, she has never been wrong before

and I trust Elizabeth's judgment."

"We have our orders. We are to remain put until E-vac arrives; I am not

jeopardizing this mission." McGuire states.

Elizabeth laughs out loud. "What mission? There is no mission Captain,

wake up. The world has gone to shit in a handbag and no one is coming for us. Now

if you want to remain here for this so called rescue, you're more than welcome but I

am taking my chances going through that opening to find another way." Elizabeth

takes a stand mustering all the strength she has inside to persuade the Captain in

changing his mind. "Now either you're with us or you're on your own."

McGuire concedes. "Ok lady, but you better be right."

Elizabeth smiles and explains to the Captain about what she has found and

her idea. "The Mayans always built pyramids and temples that had many openings.

They consisted of many entry points and lead to safe places. If they were being attacked let's say on this side they would enter back into the temple and go to other tunnels that lead them to safety away from whatever was a threat to them. So I am sure that there is another opening elsewhere that will lead us off this ledge. What have we to lose?"

Fisher is now having second thoughts as to what Elizabeth is speaking of. "She just might have something there Sir. What could it hurt, really?"

"You see what is going on around us now. That water is going to subside to a level soon in which we will be able to access the jungle once more. I know that this entrance is one of many. We need to find a way to get out of here and to a safe place. In all the finds known to man, each Mayan temple had tunnels that ran for miles almost like a mapped city within." Elizabeth is still trying hard to convince the Captain.

David interjects in Elizabeth's explanation to help. "To which they could inevitably lead further away from the water and possible dry land. A better rendezvous point for a rescue."

"I see that class in Boston has really paid off David, I'm impressed." Elizabeth smiles at David and makes light of the situation.

McGuire just stares at the two trying so hard to convince him. "So, what you're saying is. If we go inside, the chances of getting to ground level through the tunnels in this so called temple might be miles of crawling through."

"Not crawling, Captain, walking. The tunnels in the Mayan temples are like walking in hallways. It beats sitting here waiting for a rescue that isn't going to happen." Elizabeth paces back and forth frustrated by the entire situation. "We have

nothing to lose. You see what is out there, we have nowhere to go. What do you

say?" Elizabeth has now just laid everything she has in her on the line to Captain

McGuire.

McGuire thinks for a moment looking at everyone standing there. He then

looks at Sgt. Fisher. "Fisher, break out the glow sticks pass them out." McGuire

walks over to Elizabeth and sternly makes his thoughts known. "If something starts

to go wrong we come back. Got it! We come back here."

Elizabeth reassures McGuire. "Nothing is going to happen. We're going to

be fine, you'll see."

McGuire still not too sure about this new expedition he is about to take on

looks at Fisher. "I sure hope your right Professor, I hope your right."

The team of five are now thinking of the new adventure they are about to

embark on. The entrance way to the temple is Ominous looking with all the etchings

and Hieroglyphics that have aged and faded with time. The overgrowth has hidden

this area and cradled it for many centuries keeping it a secret until now. The

Professors are excited about the find and are eager to explore what it is that lay

behind the opening to the dismay of Captain McGuire.

As the tsunami ravages the Jungle below showing no mercy, there is no other

way off the mountain they have climbed that has now shown its reality of being a

Mayan Temple. History is about to be uncovered, bringing the past to the present as

the five have gone from finding a safe place of refuge to an exploration of a new

find.

Robbie Thomas

Time Shift – The Paradigm

Michael is very anxious in entering the opening and does so slowly as he brushes aside some of the cobwebs and overgrowth still visible in the entrance. "Come on everyone watch your step." Michael slowly enters holding the flashlight in his hand peering in through the dark as David Gates is right behind him.

"Careful Michael, what do you see?" David pushes through the opening and is now standing with Michael on the inside of the temple. "Would you look at this?"

Elizabeth next to enter is very anxious to see what Michael and David are looking at. "What do you two see?" She pushes through the overgrowth into the entranceway of the temple and stops. She is amazed at all its splendor as for the first time the past is now present with the three of them gazing upon history.

McGuire and Fisher still on the outside of the temple entrance discuss what's on their minds before entering. McGuire really doesn't like the idea of leaving the plateau area that was a safe haven for them all gives Fisher some directives before they enter the temple.

"Fisher, you stay close and keep an eye on those three. We can't afford to lose anyone. Whatever you do, do not allow them to run off in some tunnel that hasn't been checked out first." McGuire checks to make sure all his equipment is secure and starts to enter the opening.

Fisher turns and looks at the tsunami that is continuing to engulf everything in its way. "I totally understand sir! Let's just hope they know what they are doing." Fisher follows Captain McGuire through the opening of the temple, as now, all five are standing on the inside looking around at history.

Michael walks over to the wall, which has many hieroglyphics and pictures

Robbie Thomas

in sequence telling a story. David follows him looking at everything it has to offer. The architecture looks in pristine shape and very clear for all to see. Elizabeth stands with Captain McGuire while still trying to collect their thoughts on what they are looking at.

McGuire glances at everyone standing there and makes a request. "Ok everyone. We don't want anyone going missing or getting hurt. I suggest we stay close and whatever you do, don't wander off on your own."

"Elizabeth you have to see this come here."

Everything within the walls of this temple looks undisturbed as if it were just placed there yesterday.

"What do we have here?"

David starts to translate what is written. "Look here! The first part of what is written I believe says, 'Those who enter, are entering with the gods.' and this part here, 'from here to everlasting life with the gods.' Interesting I must say. I think we have stumbled upon something that has never been seen before on any Mayan Temple entrance."

Michael is totally amazed. "How remarkable! This is a true new discovery."

David continues to read what is written. "This other part here refers to those that do come in line from the high Priests. Look here, 'those who enter through sacrifice will live forever through the Priest of high', now this part here is a bit peculiar. Let's see. 'No one shall enter the temple without first being cleansed by the Priest. You will be damned and cursed if he, who enters, enters with no sacrifice. Death to all who enters with no blessings.' Interesting, very interesting!"

McGuire does not like what he hearing. "I told you we should've stayed out there and waited. This is not a good sign, not a good sign at all."

Elizabeth looks at McGuire and smiles. "Captain, don't tell me your scared now. It's only writing on a wall from the past." Elizabeth turns to look at more of what David is trying to translate.

"Sometimes Professor, the past comes back to haunt you. These Mayan people knew much and saw much. I don't really care to be part of the past or get caught up in it for that matter."

"Oh don't worry yourself Captain, I assure you for the most part, we have absolutely nothing to worry about. That's why they call it history; it's not of our present time. " Michael tries to reassure the Captain.

"Contrary to popular belief, I beg to differ my fine colleague." David continues to look at the writing on the wall. "Our past is our history yes, which enviably becomes part of our future."

"Are you two about done, we have to find a way out of this place." Captain McGuire looks at the two professors with a funny look. "Fisher! Find us a way out of this mess. See if you can find a way down that tunnel there, but whatever you do, don't enter a room until we are all together."

"Do you think we're going to get off this hill Captain?

"Let's hope so. We better hope they know what they are doing. I sure and hell don't want to be stuck in this dump any longer than I have to. Now let's find a way out of here."

"Yes sir. On my way."

Time Shift – The Paradigm

As history is painted on the walls of the Mayan temple, the future seems to be catching up with the team, giving indications of an impending doom. The mysterious paranormal phenomenon lends credence to the fact, our past is our history and that history repeats itself. The dark ominous flow of water, which surrounds the temple, is beckoning its call upon those who are trapped within. The utter useless feeling is now overcoming everyone who seeks a way to be saved from its ravaging way. The team desperately tries to decipher the hieroglyphics in hopes to find a way to safety. Time is not on their side, or the side of the entire world as it is running short on patience.

Robbie Thomas

The Message

The world is in dire need of a saviour, someone or something to save it from complete destruction. Global catastrophe has claimed nations, cities and people with the darkness of nevermore. Man has seen in the past how dynasties have literally disappeared, complete civilizations gone with no trace, yet the message has never been heeded to. Lessons have been inscribed on cave walls, temple stones and written in scribes of warnings, which have never been taken serious until now.

The United States is in its darkest hour, being consumed by a phenomenon unknown to man, the same phenomenon that has scoured the earth claiming its victims. The leaders of many nations worldwide have succumbed to that of which deaths door has opened. The pandemonium is a pandemic within itself, leaving people frantically trying to survive the wrath which is befalling them.

The last glimmer of hope is out there somewhere and the will of man to find it is strong. Mankind may have their backs against the wall, however, the spirit cannot be diminished whatsoever. The cries of mother earth are being heard as the last of life itself, clings to the little life line that is left.

"Mr. President. We have the Pope from the Vatican on the phone sir." Secretary Robert Sims walks into the Oval Office. "Line three Sam."

"Your Holiness. I wish we were talking at a time of better circumstances."

"Mr. President, I too wish for that, unfortunately, we are of little time and better days."

"I totally understand."

The Pope pauses and takes a deep breath. "The world is at a precipice as we both know. I am calling to give you my blessing for strength, as the people of the world are in need of hope. Gods guiding hand is here, he has not forsaken us. Listen to your heart and he will show you. May God be with you."

The President stands up from his Oval Office chair looking out the window. "May God hold you forever in his light your Holiness."

The Oval Office is dead quiet as the President turns to hang up the phone. Everyone there have their eyes trained on President Morgan as he walks around the room thinking to himself of the conversation he just had with the Pope.

"Sam we have the latest from Peru. It came in over the Satellite link up." Robert Sims walks over to the President's desk placing the data collected. "I was gathering this when the call came in from Rome."

"Have they found out anything new, what's their disposition?" The President sits to read the information.

"While evading the tsunami they made it to safer ground and were able to make a find that is of much importance with our existence. I know it may sound insane, but what they have, actually describes what we're going through now."

President Morgan looks up glancing over his glasses. "This is what we have been waiting for Robert. Have they indicated at all what we are supposed to be doing?"

"Here's the thing Sam, we were only able to receive part of the message before we lost contact. Now don't worry we're trying to establish a viable signal to get the remainder of what was coming in."

The President slams the paperwork to his desk. "Damn It Robert! Do I have

Time Shift – The Paradigm

to do this on my own? It always seems to be something screwing up. Get me that message as soon as possible."

In Owensville, things seem to be escalating in a different light. The town's folk have this collective of being serene, with a marginal feeling of fear. They are now not so apprehensive, but still very cautious of the happening not far from them. It seems to be much more of a watchful eye rather than that of a threat.

"Captain Perry, I think whatever that is out there, is most certainly not advancing on our position. We have reports of its activity being less of nature than what it was not long ago." Colonel Smith goes over the Intel given him. "I have noticed as well that the people, themselves, are complacent in a way. What do you make of that?"

"Well Sir. They seem to have accepted the fact it's there and there is nothing they can do different to make it any better than what it is," Captain Perry looks outside the tent. "That Father Murphy, he is a huge help. He seems to have things well under control with everyone going to his daily ministry. People just feel much more at ease with him."

"How's our Sheriff and his Deputy holding out?"

"Them too, they are cooperating fully with everyone, helping folks out."

"Good! Well that will be all Captain. Let me know if anything changes."

"Yes Sir!" The Captain goes to leave the tent, but stops as he has something else to tell the Colonel. "Oh Colonel, Sir, before I forget. There's this kid. It's something strange with him Sir."

"What do mean Captain?"

Robbie Thomas

"He has been seen a couple times talking to himself."

"Captain, kids do that, that's nothing new."

"No, it's different. He just doesn't talk to himself. There is this white glow around him each time he has been seen doing this."

"White glow?! Captain, you sure you know what you're telling me?"

"Yes Sir! We have watched from a distance and it's a white glow around the kid. He seems to be communicating with something or someone!"

"Keep an eye on this kid, but don't alarm the people and let me know next time this happens immediately. I want to see this for myself."

"Yes Sir."

The Captain walks out the tent to find the Sheriff because he has questions for him. As he is looking for the Sheriff he come upon Father Murphy who asks the Captain if he would be joining him tonight for mass.

"Hi Father. How are you today?"

"Doing well, my son. When was the last time you were at Mass Captain?"

"It's been a while Father, but I would love to come."

"Good! Then I will see you at seven tonight on the other side of the mess tent. Don't be late now Captain, I am counting on you."

Captain Perry decides he is going to the services at seven, for he wants to have a conversation with Father Murphy. As Mass is concluded, Captain Perry walks over to Father Murphy to discuss the little boy.

"Father, can I have word with you?"

"Most certainly, what's on your mind?"

Time Shift – The Paradigm

"The Sheriff's son. We have been watching him from a distance and noticed-"

Father Murphy interjects. "Yes!" as he describes the white light that surrounds him. He says that it's the 'man' from the other side.

"Yes. What is that?"

"Well Captain, Payton is the boys' name and he says he is able to talk to someone from the other side."

"That's just nuts Father. That can't be happening."

"Oh, but it is happening and he is doing it."

"What do they want from us Father?"

"That I don't know my son. That I don't know."

Things in Owensville for the most part, seem to be silenced and at a stalemate with the paranormal phenomena. People are taking notice of the special gift the Sheriff's son has and the way he is able to communicate with something, or someone from the other side. The mysterious ominous mirrored happening has been less active in the recent days and more of a lurking giant, watching those who are on the McKinnon Farm.

While in Peru, the waters are rising, making their way up the sides of the Mayan Temple, leaving everyone inside very nervous, for there is no way out and they are trapped. The five realize time is of the essence as they need to figure out what the message left behind many centuries ago would be the pass key to their extended existence in this life. They are franticly interpreting the hieroglyphics, but having difficulty solving the puzzle left from the past. They are in satellite hook-up

Robbie Thomas

with the White House relaying messages back and forth with the President and his staff.

"Michael, do you remember when we were in the Caves in Brazil? There were pictures that were different from the hieroglyphs that were etched there. These seem to be the same and the way they are placed here too."

"Yes, I think your right!"

Sgt. Fisher establishes Satellite connection with the White House. "Captain! We're in. I got connection sir."

"Good. I don't know how long we have with this signal Professors, so we better transmit whatever you have as soon as you can." Captain McGuire informs David and Michael.

"Come in…Come in. This is Professor David Gates-"

"No need for that Professor they can hear you and see you, just tell them what is going on." Sgt. Fisher explains.

"Ok. Over here on this wall we have many hieroglyphics that explain the coming of this time we are in now. The way they convey their message is through two separate languages. One common known historical writing, and one that I am having difficulty decoding."

Elizabeth speaks up. "David is that not a time reference in this mid-sentence of what they are trying to say. I can make that out!"

"Yes I think your right. Ok, Mr. President as you see the time line reference given here it says…let me see. Yes it does say the year in which this is now and wait! It also says there will be a time of tranquility."

Robbie Thomas

Time Shift – The Paradigm

The signal from the satellite hook-up becomes very weak and the connection is lost to the White House. Everyone on both ends are frantically trying to re-establish the link.

"We're trying to fix the link up Mr. President; it will be just a moment sir." White House Chief of Staff Anne Reynolds it trying to get the signal back. "It shouldn't be much longer."

"We really need to find out what is written on those walls. We don't have much time people, get me that satellite hook-up now!"

"We're back up but the signal is weak. I don't know how long we have but we're back on." Robert Sims is anxiously waiting for the transmission. "It just takes a second here Sam, and we will be connected. There we go, we're in!"

The President of the United States immediately starts to ask questions of the professors. "Ok people we don't have much time and I don't know how long our connection is going to last, so if you will please, continue in what you were telling us."

Professor Gates continues what he was saying. "Right you are. Ok, Mr. President like I was saying the writings are of different origin not from the Mayan era or time at all. Now I can't be certain sir as to where they come from but they are of a different dialect. This makes is a bit tougher to interpret, but I am going to do my best."

"Ready when you are Professor, do what you do."

"Over here on this wall, we have established a time line as previously talked about, but the rest of this on the wall is troublesome to me. I am having a bit of difficulty understanding what is said." David walks over shinning more light on the wall. "If I can just…" He reaches up to brush away some of the collected dust on the wall. "There that's better. Ok, what we have is something to me that looks like they might be talking about a resurrection of some sort. I could be mistaken, I am not sure."

Elizabeth walks a bit closer, looking harder at the markings. As she reads what is there, she steps back realizing what is written. "David! I think I know what this means!" Elizabeth is excited as she not only feels, but she knows what is written. "Mr. President! I know what it is! What they are trying to tell us is, we all need-"

Just as Professor Ross is about to explain what is said on the wall, a huge earthquake starts to rumble shaking the temple violently. The satellite hook-up is catching this as it transmits back to the White House. Everyone in the Oval Office is witnessing the temple starting to crumble and cave in from the force of the earthquake. The water starts to rush in cutting transmission as the laptop shorts out. The temple has now collapsed under the dark waters that surrounded it. The team in Peru have lost their lives trying to save the rest of the world, but have failed to relay the message needed for mankind.

"Oh my god!" White House Chief of Staff Anne Reynolds can't believe what she along with the others have just witnessed. "They're gone! Now what are we going to do?"

The President sits back in his chair with a blank stare on his face. "May God help us all."

Robbie Thomas

Time Shift – The Paradigm

Vice President Donald Reese enters the room with information of yet another satellite link up, but this time from Owensville Kansas. He walks over to the President whispering in his ear about the communication coming in.

"We have a live feed coming to us from Owensville Kansas."

"Owensville Kansas? What, or better yet, who is in Owensville Kansas that are trying to reach us? Is this a joke!?"

"No Joke, I think you better take this!"

The President looks really puzzled as to who would be trying to contact the White House from a small farming town in Kansas.

"Sam! I really think you should take this."

"Ok Donald, this better be good."

Donald Reese asks Anne Reynolds to connect to the link up putting it on one of the big screens in the Oval Office.

"Colonel Smith, can you hear us and see us?"

"Yes Sir Mr. Vice President. We can see and hear you sir."

"Good. Now can you tell the President exactly what you have explained to me just a moment a go?"

"Mr. President. We might have an answer to what is going on around the world sir. There seems to be a type of connection that a little boy here has with whatever that is doing this."

The President sits up listening attentively to what the Colonel has to say. "What your trying to tell me is that a little boy has some type of inside connection to this phenomena!?"

Robbie Thomas

Time Shift – The Paradigm

"That's exactly it sir!"

"Can you tell me Colonel and now I am very interested to know, but what exactly is that connection?"

"He says he talks to a man from the other side Sir. I know that sounds crazy, but I have seen some type of real anomaly happening between this little boy and whatever he says he is talking to."

"What exactly have you seen Colonel?"

"Well Sir, it's just not me many people here have witnessed it. It's a white glow around the boy when he says he is talking to this man. He says he has a message for all of us."

The President pauses for a brief moment collecting his thoughts. "Ok Colonel what's the message?"

"He won't tell me sir. He says he has to talk to you and only you."

"Let me talk to the boy Colonel!"

"Yes Sir."

The Colonel waves the little boy over in front of the satellite hook-up so he can be seen and heard.

"Hello Son. What's your name?"

"Payton!"

"Ok Payton. This is the President. Do you know who I am?"

"Yes, mommy says you're a man who lives in a white house."

"Why yes Payton she's right. Payton, can you tell me who this man is that you talk to?"

Robbie Thomas

"He says we all need to pray more. He says we all have to be nicer to each other."

"Why does he say that, Payton?"

"He says we all have to be good to each other."

"Payton where does this man come from, can you tell me?

"He comes from the other side. He says it's nice there."

"Ok Payton I'm going to ask you a very important question and I want you to give me answer. Did this man tell you how we can stop the bad stuff going on in the world?"

"He has a message for the world."

The President looks over at his Vice President telling him to broadcast this on all open channels for the Nation as well as all world media.

"We don't need to, his voice is being heard everywhere!"

"What do you mean heard everywhere!?"

The Vice President walks over to the Oval Office Window and opens it. "Listen, its coming from everywhere!"

The President looks directly at the camera to Payton. "Payton, can you tell me the message?"

A voice not of the boy starts to speak. It emanates in a tone of an adult coming through the child. Everyone in the Oval Office is stunned at what is being said. This is being heard out around the world, for the world to see as finally a message from beyond is being given.

"Humanity as you know it to be, is a selfish benign civilization of many separate nations fighting each other, hurting one another for too long. Leaving those

to hunger and thirst while many feed on greed and gluttony. Leaders of these nations

fail to make peace and would rather create wars of destruction and poverty among

weaker nations. The evil that men do is the doing of their own hands. You all have

failed to see and take heed to the message passed down from the beginning of time.

Mother Earth cries out as you are contaminating her. The people of this world are

blind to what goes on around them. You, who are listening, must change, for the

change comes from within. It's not a world of many nations, but a world of one race.

Man has to be kind to one another as you have faltered in faith. You must now

restore faith in man and man in his faith.

The little boy that was talking from spirit has now stopped. The spirit within

him, just stares into the camera as this is heard all over the world. Nations fall to

their knees, while news broadcasts around the world see people in Europe, Africa,

Australia, The Middle East, South America, Asia, and America all begin to pray as

one people, one race. The magnitude of prayer along with goodwill from all men as

one race can be felt in harmony finally, which transcends throughout the Time Shift.

This is what was needed to save man from himself.

The Change is up to all of us!

Robbie Thomas

Critic Reviews of Time Shift

"This Book Is EPIC!"

Robbie Thomas's book "Time Shift : The Paradigm" is an *astounding roller-coaster* ride through an exciting world that I walk away feeling personally invested in. Robbie takes a very cerebral approach to writing that informs with legitimate fact and current research while keeping the action *extremely exciting* and pulls you more into the world he writes about. Time Shift is written in a way that you become immersed in the story, you understand the motives and thoughts of the characters, you start to care and worry about them. It becomes so easy to relate to with the inclusion of fact and current theories that you can visualize yourself involved with the story. But just when you start to understand what's happening... *WHAM!*... there's another curve ball that takes you down another exciting path full of science, twists, turns, reality and surreal moments of unexplained phenomena and so much more!

This is a book that is extremely hard to put down! Part of me knows it's fiction but then again, frequently you are left thinking about the possibility of....I just can't give it away! You must read this to understand. When one chapter ends you drive to know what happens next. Robbie's writing brings surreal phenomena to a level that makes you think it could be an extreme possibility in reality. I am thoroughly excited to review this book for Robbie Thomas and I eagerly anticipate more great writings! "

Robbie Thomas

Side Note:

All that aside I have one specific scene that is still haunting me from last night. The part between Zebra Station and the #2 Pod I believe....That writing is so exciting I'm heavily reminded of The Airport Scene in Stephen Kings The Langoliers. The reason I make that comparison is that is absolutely one of my favorite books and it was represented well in movie form. I make this coloration because it is EXTREMELY Easy to see this book in movie form and I would be extremely excited to hear that as a possibility too!

Michael Kalinowski

Review Critic for Schiffer Pulishing

Paranormal Researcher/Investigator/Show host

Visions Into The Past - Paranormal Radio

Robbie Thomas

"Robbie has outdone himself with his novel about parallel worlds! With catastrophic events taking place around the world, a team of experts is sent to investigate something even science can't explain. I couldn't help but wonder if the story was based on vivid imagination or insights into the future of our world colliding with a parallel world.."

Dr. Sharon Oester PHD

Coyote Moon Publishing

International Ghost Hunter Society

"Your book is such an exciting piece of work! I like your writing style- it's simple, lucid yet engaging and builds up the suspense and drama effectively. It also deals with how our beliefs in the existence of the Spirit and its Realms are reflected in the courses of action that has to take to wake us up and get our perspectives sorted. The reader gets to glean all this through thrills and suspense till the book ends. Another compelling and heartfelt novel from the man who has access to The Other Side!"

Mrs Sudakshina Bhattacharjee (nee Mukherjee)

Journalist, Lecturer, Author and Poet

"Robbie Thomas' Time Shift - The Paradigm, is a master piece of work blending

Robbie Thomas

fiction and non-fiction to create a suspenseful read that is destined to become a best

seller! As I read through each chapter, I stay riveted on every word of this page

turner. I can only imagine how this would play out as a film on the big screen! This

book is another MUST READ, from one of my favourite authors."

Bob Davis

Planet Paranormal Broadcast Entertainment Network

*"One thing I can say is, **THIS BOOK IS OFF THE HOOK!*** Some parts I had to

read twice ONLY because I had the 'did that really just happen, did I really read

that! ' The action, and suspense is just off the wall. A Best Seller all the way!"

Mike Carson

Rock 106/Sunny 98/The Wolf 92.3 Managing Partner of GiMase Media

Robbie Thomas

Other Book's By Robbie

Paranormal Encounters

'Paranormal Encounters', is a complete, comprehensive, behind-the-scenes look at paranormal investigations and at two major movies, 'The Sallie House', and the critically acclaimed hit movie 'Dead Whisper' where first-time-ever communications with the other side was captured in direct conversations with a psychic medium. You are going to be captivated by what the other side has to say as Robbie Thomas brings forward more than just validation that was caught on EVP and film but the truth behind each place visited on this journey. The uninvited were most prevalent during these many factual moments that were all documented in real time, either on film, electronic voice phenomena, or written documentation in script form. As you read through these chilling accounts, you will become more than entranced...you will be living 'The Dead Whisper'!

"The books is great! I really did enjoy reading it, this is excellent." - Barrie John, Award Winning Psychic Television Personality, England

"Paranormal Encounters is *definitely the best-selling book for 2010!!!* I could not put this book down." -Carmela Giorgio, Perth Australia

"Paranormal Encounters is well worth reading and including in your paranormal library. It is 195 pages of information and enlightenment into the spirit world and

Robbie Thomas

someone who can see and hear what most of us can only wonder about. Although *Ghost* was only a Hollywood representation of fictional characters, **_Robbie Thomas and Paranormal Encounters is the real deal!_** -Drs. Dave DD, PhD, Reiki Master and Sharon Oester PhD, International Ghost Hunters Society

Signs From Heaven

Robbie Thomas, world-renowned medium psychic, has been helping people around the world for many years bringing them closer to the other side through contact with their loved ones. As you read Signs from Heaven, you are taking an enlightening journey, giving you much more perspective of life on the other side and within you. You are going to witness many accounts that are verified by testimonials from many individuals from around the world. Each account is different, giving much weight to the validity within! This book has been craved for a long while, finally coming to light to share in the very essence of spirit it was meant for, and the realm of spirit of you. Please sit back, letting the truth of spirit surround you, allowing yourself to embrace everything within. Signs from Heaven, is thought provoking while leaving the reader wanting much more. It is the fire that burns within, the yearning to learn, the quest for knowledge that we seek, so grab hold of this beautifully written account of factual writings and find the solace you seek!

"I wish you all the success with this endeavor. **_This is a truly inspiring story!_**" - Roger Gallaway, PC, MP Federal Government Official of Canada

Robbie Thomas

"I didn't want this book to end! Robbie Thomas words permeated my very existence and were indelibly inscribed in my mind. For you are a true 'pillar of light', a messenger of God!" - Reverend May Leilani Schmidt, Spiritual Healer

To You From Spirit

Uplifting and well written in reflection for the soul! Everyone who reads this book will carefully place a bookmarker within his or her heart, which will give abundant solace within. The writing is that of great origin, the finest in the guidance from spirit to which each who turns the pages will be exuberant with enlightenment. Each page grows with you as you are drawn into the spiritual uplifting element of this book. Without further ado, allow yourself to feel whole in spirit when the message is To You From Spirit.

"In modern times rarely does an author mesh the factual strength of hard science with uplifting beauty of pure spirituality. *One thing I can guarantee is that you will be a much different person when you start reading this book* from the one you' ll become once you've finish"
-Michael Esposito, EVP Researcher/Paranormal Investigator

"Robbie Thomas has changed my life! This book and his teachings have changed a lot in me and the way I look at things. I am sure if you read this book, you too will

Robbie Thomas

Time Shift – The Paradigm

find what you are looking for!"

-Trevor "Moose" Stoyko, Radio DJ Bob Fm

For more information about Robbie Thomas visit www.robbiethomas.net

Robbie Thomas

Robbie Thomas

Made in the USA
Charleston, SC
24 May 2012